Robbed of a Childhood, Raped by the System

Thanks so much for your
Support.

Sunny Bane

Robbed of a Childhood, Raped by the System

✦

Autobiography of an Adult Survivor of Child Abuse

BY Sunny Love

iUniverse, Inc.

New York Lincoln Shanghai

Robbed of a Childhood, Raped by the System
Autobiography of an Adult Survivor of Child Abuse

iUniverse books may be ordered through booksellers or by contacting:

iUniverse
2021 Pine Lake Road, Suite 100
Lincoln, NE 68512
www.iuniverse.com
1-800-Authors (1-800-288-4677)

The views expressed in this work are solely those of the author and do not necessarily reflect the views of the publisher, and the publisher hereby disclaims any responsibility for them.

Edited by Julie Tilka

ISBN: 978-0-595-44723-7 (pbk)
ISBN: 978-0-595-89044-6 (ebk)

Printed in the United States of America

Contents

Acknowledgements

Thank you, my Lord and my children. Without their love, I wouldn't be here writing this book.

Many thanks also to my friend, Julie, who put in countless hours editing this book. We had been friends for years when I read her my story. When I read what I had endured as a child, she started to cry. I said, "Don't cry, Julie, because I have lived through the pain and the shame, and today I am writing this book from the heart so others might know we can overcome."

To my husband and confidant, I share my heart with you. This book has taken seven long years for me to publish. Not publishing it right away was out of fear of what the world might think of me. My story is best told than untold, especially for the millions of women, men and children who live with the same shame.

Today I say this to the world: Live and be free of all the shame hidden in the crevices of your mind. The enemy still lies in those crevices, ready to rob you of your joy. I feel a freedom today that I would never have believed possible as a child, and especially as an adult who fought off panic attacks for eight years. At one point in my life, they came so frequently that I believed I was going to stop breathing. It was a relief when a doctor in an emergency room at County Medical Center told me the worst thing that could happen during attacks was that I would black out. He said my brain would still send signals for my body to continue breathing. I researched what caused panic attacks, and I worked through them with therapy and much reading and learning.

To my brother, Bennie: Thank you from the bottom of my heart. Without your constant nagging for me to get this book out, it would have never happened.

He is the first person the Lord reeled in as the watchman of my soul through his prayers. There were times he phoned me to let me know he was worried about me getting murdered out there in that world. Instead of heeding his warnings, I would say, "Bennie, don't preach to me. I don't hear you. I know what I am doing and I am careful."

Thank you, Bennie, from the bottom of my heart for your never-ending love for me. You have all of my love and support in your own journey through life.

To all of the men, women and youth who have afforded me an opportunity to work with, you are the ones who have been a blessing in my life. So many times you believed I was helping to save you, but it was only through your honest testimonies that I feel inspired and more complete in my work. We will win this battle with the system. You will be able to share your stories of pain, shame and hidden secrets, because you know freedom has to come from within before you can truly live again. Be encouraged, never give up or give in, and know I am always here for you.

I am also sending a note of appreciation to the Mothers of my church, Greater St. Paul Church of God in Christ. Because of their love, I have been inspired to remain committed to being a light for other women, men and children, so they know that we can change our direction in life and love doing it at the same time. Life away from the streets and saunas is a blessing and, for the first time in my life, I feel worthy of being loved. And, thank you, Pastor Vernell Thomas for being the upright man you are and for living your faith.

Finally, I would like to thank the therapist at County Medical Center who's intense compassion for my well being made me want to open up all the way. She helped me believe I could be free of the ghosts from my past. For once in my life, I could be free to love with an open heart. No longer could my shameful childhood memories rob me of the life I so richly deserved. Thank you so very much.

The names of people used in this book have been changed to protect their privacy.

Introduction

Throughout most of my life, I wondered why I turned out the way I did. After working through all of the mess that was my life, today I really believe I get it. You see, oftentimes we don't see or explore our own insecurities to any depth, while we can easily point out the flaws of our loved ones, neighbors and anyone else who might cross our paths.

Today I work with men, women and youth exiting correctional institutions. I love doing this work. It has afforded me an opportunity to work with people at depth to help them unearth their potential, and it has helped me to look at my own flaws and embrace the work I need to do in my own life.

For the past four years, I have worked to create an organization called Women Planting Seeds. The goal of this organization is to allow a person who has served their time to come back into society. Men and women exiting corrections are humans who have hope for their future, unless the system has dehumanized them. There are so many young people incarcerated for getting high on drugs. This is a disgrace to the liberty we claim to give to all people in this country. People are hurting and what do we do? We hurt them more by putting them in prison and then cutting them loose without the proper support. People get high for a reason. Why not treat their pain rather than helping to increase it?

All of us want dignity in our lives, but some are robbed of their dignity by the system. I know because I lived through a crooked bust and a brutal criminal justice system. When it happened, I felt empty and unworthy of life. Today I know there is a life after the abuse and denial. No one could have told me this then. At the time, I was one of the living dead.

Now as an advocate, I have worked for many years with "those people" and found that they know how to be real because that is all they have done most of their lives. So many of us pretend that we are something we aren't just to satisfy our image of how we should be in this world. After scraping by trying to make a dime and surviving abuse, "those people" don't have to put up any front. They have had to be about as real as it gets. How can you learn to be anything else when your life has been so confusing and distorted?

Some decide to live within a make-believe view on life. I prefer to see life as it is. Don't kid yourself: Life in prison is no picnic. In our country today we have more people in prison than in any other nation on earth: over two million. In Michigan, there are over forty-two prisons and in Wisconsin, thirty-one. Here in Minnesota, we have eight prisons with more than 8,000 inmates. Our prison population has increased 45 percent in five short years.

What is wrong with this picture? Or what is right with it in your eyes? I leave this for you to ponder. I will continue to serve the needs of those less fortunate.

As a support organization, Women Planting Seeds might not have a lot of dollars, but we have a lot of love. We aren't able to serve as many as some organizations, but we truly serve more than many others. Women Planting Seeds facilitates adult and youth circles of support; leads self-esteem and healthy relationships training and conducts domestic violence workshops.

I wish for all of you to be blessed, be encouraged and never give up.

1

Childhood Memories ... and Nightmares

As a child I was not very proud of my life.

Starting at a point in my life that I can remember, I remember the day my mother decided to marry a man named Harry Creep. He was a tall, large brown-skinned man, very good-looking—at least to some who knew him. He had three sons ranging from sixteen through twenty years old, and one daughter named Ann, the oldest of the bunch.

Before my mother married Harry I remember us being so happy-go-lucky, sharing a house with my great-grandmother, my mother, my brother, my little sister and I. We sometimes got into trouble with mom. She would go out to do things mothers have to do to parent her children and leave us with our great-grandmother. Our great-grandmother was somewhat crippled and couldn't get around very well, so watching my brother and I was hard for her. One day my mother was gone and we somehow found an ice pick and we poked holes in 89 cans of peaches. That was just one of the mischievous things we did.

I also remember my mother being gone another time and my baby sister fell behind the bed. My great-grandmother was caring for her and when momma arrived back home my sister was dead from suffocation. This was a horrifying event for us to experience. I don't believe I ever got over the pain, I just hid it deep down inside. I don't remember much about my real father before my mother married Harry.

My mother was a thin black woman about five feet three inches tall and one hundred fifteen pounds with medium-length black hair. Everyone in this small country town objected to my mother marrying Harry. Love does strange things even to the best of us. People tried to tell my mother how mysteriously his first wife had died, but she did not want to listen. No one could tell her anything negative about my stepfather. Well, they could, but it didn't have any impact on how she felt about him. She was so blinded by his smooth-talking ways she couldn't really hear what was being said to her. As you may well imagine, my mother went ahead and married this man. Little did she know that it was the beginning of the end for her.

We moved to Harry's farm in Henderson, Tennessee into a very large house, which was kind of scary. I remember I was always afraid to be alone in that old house, because the walls were always squeaking and sounds came from every direction. My heart would race and pound as if it would jump right out of my little six-year-old chest.

For me, the nightmare began on day two on that farm. That day my stepbrother Willie waited for the others to leave for work to hoe cotton in Mr. Berry's fields. After everyone was gone from the house, he began to undress me. Willie did not ask my permission to undress me he just pulled my clothes off and the ordeal began. After undressing me, he made me lie down and he forced his large penis inside of me. I remember the pain being so unbearable I thought I would black out. It was just excruciating. I had to endure his nasty smelling odious body on top of me.

I couldn't understand why he would do something like this to me. Mom had told me he was my brother now and I should love him as a real brother. Yet Mom wasn't here to hear my cries of agony. There was no one to cry out to but the Lord. We were located too far away from civilization to run next door for help. Our nearest neighbors were miles away so it was too far to run or walk. Everyone else was at Mr. Berry's farm hoeing or picking cotton.

When everyone returned from the fields, I was too petrified to tell my mother. I didn't have the guts. I was afraid to tell anyone because Willie said no one would believe me anyway. I thought to myself that I must be a coward because I was too ashamed to let anyone know what had happened to me.

Willie would come onto me whenever he could figure out an excuse to stay on the farm. He would take me to buy some candy when we were in town. He actually believed this would make everything all right. What a joke! I thought that my mother might just believe him if he said I was lying. "Mom knows little girls tend to exaggerate things," he'd say to me. Willie also said to me that she would say that, "I asked for it." As a child, it made me wonder if maybe he was right.

I didn't understand what was happening to me, and I even began to think that what he was doing to me felt good. And there were times that I felt this meant he really cared about me. I couldn't rid myself of the shame that came to mind when all I truly desired was to feel loved. Deep down I knew that this could not be love. It was too demented to be the kind of satisfaction one feels when they are in love with a boy or man.

I was at a loss as to whom I could talk to about what was being done to me. I was so afraid that momma would hate me for not stopping what was happening. My mother and I were so close. She had taught me how to cook when I was just four years old. Standing in a chair over the stove, I would prepare the meals for the twelve of us.

We shared four beds (boys and girls) and I believe this is what started a lot of the incest problems. Most nights one of the boys or girls would urinate and some of us would get wet. The wetness felt so darn nasty. Just the smell was enough to make me sick. How disgusting it was for us to have to endure. After waking up in urine, I would jump out of the bed and ask who did it. Everyone was afraid to answer for fear they would be beaten. We were accustomed to getting whipped for almost everything we did wrong. We became afraid of owning up to our mistakes.

I remember thinking one day how nice it would be just to have my own bed. I knew that was probably many light years away, but dreams are sometimes all you have.

My stepbrother Raymond was the oldest of the boys and I felt much closer to him, because he didn't hurt me like Willie did. I often found myself feeling as though I had a crush on him, but I would fight off those feelings, knowing it was not good to feel that way about him because he was my stepbrother. Raymond had never touched me in a bad way; his playfulness was for fun. He was very nice to me and he always made me feel special.

One evening he came home drunk. He was very upset with his girlfriend for breaking up with him. The more we talked about it, the more upset he became. I tried to change the subject, but he wanted to wallow in his sorrow. How could he expect me to comprehend what he was sharing with me, I was only seven years old? Finally, he told me to shut up and to get the hell out of his face. I started to cry. He asked me to come over and sit on his lap. I was hesitant at first because of what Willie had done to me in the past, but I really liked Raymond.

Trusting anyone was a hard task, yet I thought Raymond would never hurt me. Oh boy, how wrong could a child have been?

When I sat on his lap, he pulled my panties down. I started to cry. He said, "Do not cry, I will be gentle. I will not hurt you, just trust me." I wanted so bad to trust him, so I took a chance. Anyway, why not trust him? Why assume he would hurt me as Willie did. A part of me wanted to see what he was going to do to me. I was curious what it would be like if he touched me.

Raymond raised my dress and he started licking me between my legs. It didn't hurt and I started to like it. Yet I knew it was wrong, because he was my stepbrother, so I cried out to him to stop because I didn't want him to do this to me. I felt it shouldn't be happening and I was feeling so nasty and ashamed. After he was done licking me, he got some oil and rubbed my vagina. Then pulled out his penis and he rammed it into me. I cried out in agony because it hurt so badly.

I didn't believe that Raymond was different than Willie anymore, because they both had taken advantage of me and had hurt me deeply. It felt as if someone had stabbed a knife between my legs. I was screaming for dear life, but no one heard my cries. I began to bleed a lot. Still he refused to stop. He just kept on forcing himself inside of me. Finally he ejaculated and rolled off the top of me. I ran into the bedroom to clean myself up before anyone arrived home from the fields. He told me that I should not be ashamed of what he had done, because brothers and sisters loved one another and that was all right. I told him I would not tell anyone what he had done to me. Anyway, I was too devastated to say anything.

As a child the shame was so overwhelming I didn't desire to share it with anyone. And sometimes even though it was painful, it was better than being beaten or watching my mother being abused.

2

Saturday Night Fights

Later that summer when my stepfather was sharecropping for Mr. Berry's farm, my mother pulled a disk in her back while picking cotton in the fields. When she got home she went straight to bed. She awakened hours later in great pain. We pleaded to her to go to the doctor, but she refused to do so and as time passed her condition became much more serious.

My mother had caused extensive damage to her back while picking cotton. After her injury, Harry Creep and my mother started going out at night a lot. My mother went out to hide her agony from the pain she was experiencing. My step-father went out just because he liked the taste of alcohol. He seemed to like the way it made him feel.

I guess it was because he felt so strong when he drank that he would always beat my mom. My stepfather was always accusing my mother of being at fault for some guy flirting with her. My mother adored this worthless man and I knew that she would not purposely draw attention to herself. She never left the farm without my stepfather, so she never even had a chance to think about being unfaithful.

It was always very late when they got back home. My stepfather and mother would come home and the fighting would begin. My stepfather would beat my mother really bad. I called my aunt for help but she told me to go to bed. I would tell her that I was not going to bed, because I wanted him to leave my mother alone. I disliked my aunt for not helping my mother. If my stepfather wouldn't stop beating my mother, I would run from my room screaming at my stepfather. There were times I believed that he would kill her, and no one would be the wiser.

Harry Creep was a very bad person, and I wanted desperately for someone to find out this was happening and to take him to jail. I even wondered why my mother didn't just leave this asshole. Yet it is not that easy to run when you live in the country. He continued to beat her all over the house. She never had the opportunity to get very far. After he was through kicking my mom's ass, he would tire of fighting and go to bed exhausted.

I would lie there in my bed trembling, wanting to comfort my mother but afraid of what the consequences might be. So my real brother, Toby, and I would cuddle next to each other to feel safe. We would experiment with one another sexually. There were times after being sexually molested by my stepbrothers that I knew fondling one another felt better than hearing our mother being abused. We began to think it was okay to do this sort of thing.

The following morning I would wonder why my mother acted like nothing had happened the night before. This was another unanswered question in my life....

One Friday night I remember him beating her so bad that I leapt on his back and tried to bite his neck. He just slung me across the room like a rag doll. When he did this my mother ran into the kitchen, grabbed a butcher knife and stabbed it deep into his stomach. She pulled down on the knife and gutted him as if she were gutting a hog. Blood was everywhere, but I didn't feel any sorrow for him. She should have gotten him back a long time ago. But momma rushed to his aid and wrapped him with a towel and drove him to the hospital.

Unfortunately, the asshole lived and was back home within three days. And as usual, the abuse continued. I wished he had died. During the course of all this fighting, I learned to hate the sight of blood and I start to shake every time someone fights. My body trembles all over when I see someone bleeding, and I quiver and shake like Jell-o. I also learned to hate the smell of alcohol at a very young age, because I associated alcohol with violent outbursts.

I became aggressive and would often get into fights with my brothers even though I knew I couldn't win. How can a child learn to be normal in this type of environment? Especially when he or she never sees anyone being normal, except on the TV show, "Father Knows Best." We all knew that show was not real, but it never hurt to pretend.

There was all kinds of swearing in the house—enough to make me think those bad words were normal vocabulary. I started using the same language as my siblings and parents. Using vulgar words made me feel powerful for once in my life.

One day as I was running through the woods and cut my foot badly on a broken bottle. The blood was gushing out everywhere and a numbing feeling came over my foot. I ran into the house and called out to my mother. She came running out to me, picked me up and ran with me in her arms into the kitchen. Momma grabbed a pail of cold water and she put my foot into the water. I watched the water turn red as an apple and I almost blacked out from the panic. She grabbed a towel and wrapped my foot with it. When the bleeding stopped, she peeled a potato and scraped the flesh from the potato and applied a bandage to hold the potato against my cut. The next morning my wound was closed and no flesh was showing. It was as if it had been stitched with cat's guts without the dots. My mom had a lot of old home remedies for healing colds and healing up large cuts and wounds.

My mother finally went to the doctor about her back injury from years before due to picking cotton in the fields, because she could no longer endure the pain. The doctor told her he wished that she had come to him sooner. Because she had waited so long, he explained, her injury had developed into cancer on her spine. The spinal column is so thin that when cancer attaches itself there isn't much room for operating—or for hope. My mother arrived back home saddened. She was only 34 years old at the time and the mother of eight children.

The doctor told her to get things in order. He told her she only had two years at most to live. This wasn't much time to figure out what to do about your eight children, and all being so young. I was the oldest at the time and I was only nine years old. My mother sat me down and she talked with me a lot. She wanted to cram a lifetime of knowledge into my small brain. I adored her so very much. I thought she was so brave.

My mother had never had a life of her own: always picking cotton, or hoeing cotton, or taking care of us kids. She never had had a chance to see anything. My mother never left Tennessee to my knowledge. I used to ask God to please take me instead of my mother. She had so many kids, I wanted her to live and be able to see them grow up.

Even though she had so many things to see and do, I guess it just was her time to go to heaven. She never had a life anyway, so what did he take, nothing. I knew mom would be better off without all the pain. We prayed together that God would come and take her to a better place. Momma had been bedridden for such a long time, even before the cancer. Before her illness she had been such a lively woman—full of life. It was so hard to see her in this condition. Momma was one of the strongest women I have ever known.

One day, momma was so sick that she stayed in bed all day long. Willie took advantage of this moment to carry me outside to his dad's car. He had to have his way with me and he didn't care whether my mother was home or not. She was asleep and couldn't help me even if she woke up because she was too weak.

This time when Willie started having intercourse with me I began to like the way it made me feel, because it wasn't as painful as it had been before. When he was done he told me that I had caused him to get into trouble with my mother, which is why he had to punish me. I never told him that I was no longer mad about it. The pain was not as bad as it had been in the past and it made me feel good. But the shame that came from the experience was devastating.

When my mother first met Harry, his sons, including Raymond were already in their late teens and early twenties. They all knew better. This was really rape. After Raymond was done using me, he left me outside in the dark alone and I was truly afraid. It was dark in those woods surrounding our house. I eventually found my way back into the house and went to bed. I was glad momma was asleep and didn't even realize I had been outside.

I would tell myself over and over that Willie would be punished for what he had done to me. God would someday punish him for his wrongdoings.

My mother was only able to lie around and cry most of the time, because her pain was so unbearable. She screamed for my step-grandfather to give her some of her pain medicine. When she ran out of her pain medicine, he shot rubbing alcohol into her veins. Momma started having episodes that caused her to violently shake all over. It is my belief that the rubbing alcohol was causing these seizures. It was also my belief that my step-grandfather was helping kill her. One day I told him to stop shooting rubbing alcohol into her veins or I would call my aunt and tell her. He told me to just be quiet and he knew what to do to stop her pain. He said to me, "You're was just a snot-nosed kid who doesn't know shit, and that if you know what was good for you, you would shut the hell up." How I prayed that someone would come and save her from this hellhole she was in.

I watched my mother turn into a vegetable right before my eyes. I had so much hurt and no one to talk to but the Lord, so I prayed that the Lord would take my mother away. The pain was too severe for her to withstand any longer. I felt she would be much better off in heaven. Earth just seemed so darn cruel.

My momma died shortly after two years since her cancer diagnosis. This was not before she had taken time to write my aunt a letter. The letter stated that my stepbrothers and my stepfather were having their way with me. My mother wanted my birth father to be notified of the situation. She asked that on the day of her death that my father come for my brother and myself. The day she died my father arrived to take us to Indianapolis, Indiana.

It really shocked me to learn that my mother had seen what my stepbrothers and my stepfather had been doing to me. When my stepfather raped me, it was so disgusting that I never wanted to remember it. I always tried to push it out of my mind. All I remembering is that I used to pray all the time that the Lord would someday let him die for hurting me this way. I never knew until the letter that she had known. The Lord protected me from this revelation. I don't feel that I would have been able to endure what I did, had I known all along that my mother knew what was happening to me.

As a child I had always believed it was my mother's job to protect me from all harm and danger. Even though I knew she was too weak to help me, I would have still been very upset with her if I had known she had been compliant.

I didn't know much about my real father, Lenny, except that I remembered him coming to the farm for visits. He would visit my mother and give her money to help support us. After he left, my stepfather would always beat my mother for taking the money he gave her for my brother and me. For this reason alone, I didn't like my real father. He didn't know that my stepfather was beating my mother, because she never told him.

My father refused to let me attend my mother's funeral because he said I was too young to understand what had happened. I hated my father for not letting me go to my mother's funeral. I felt I was never able to say good-bye to her. I just wanted to tell her that I loved her and that I would be good so I could see her in heaven one day.

Before we left I had asked my stepfather to give me the only picture he had of my mother. He refused my request, saying he didn't have any more pictures of her. I left that farm devastated without even a picture of my mom to glance at. No one can ever take away the memories, but my heart still cries out to have just a picture of her close by at all times.

3

The Little Angel and Her Wicked Stepmother

I never had a childhood because I was taught to be a mother at a very young age. My responsibility was to help my momma raise my sisters and brothers. After leaving that farm all I could think about was who would take care of them now. I had to leave behind six siblings: four sisters and two brothers. Henry was the oldest boy on my mothers' side. Tom was the next in line, then Sherry, Sara, Ruby and Denise. These were my half brothers and sisters; they had the same mother but different fathers. My half brothers and sisters weren't allowed to leave Tennessee when my father came and got my brother and I and took us to Indianapolis.

Toby was my blood brother—he and I had the same mother and father. Even though we are the only two who are biological by both my real father and my mother, we were all raised never to make a distinction between "brothers and sisters", because we all lived together and loved each other in our own (sometimes weird) ways.

No one knew how deep my burdens felt to me. God knew because I prayed to him daily for peace of mind. He was my only source of strength and protection. I was considered mom's little caretaker of the house. That's why, when my father took me to Indianapolis, Indiana, I was filled with so much sorrow and anger. What he didn't understand was that I had been a mother to my brother and sisters for so long. When I left they had no protection whatsoever. Harry Creeps' sons were like animals without cages, yet I could not bring myself to tell my father what I had gone through because I felt it was none of his business. After all, he was a man, and I had come to the conclusion that men were not to be trusted.

I wasn't able to put my trust in anyone, especially another man. Men were really considered my enemies, and not to be trusted any farther than they could be seen. I was forced to move into a situation that I didn't want to be in. I built my own fantasy world to deal with what might be happening to my younger sisters and it tore me apart. I thought I had to be strong to carry on or I would die, and strong so no one in this new household would harm me. I was so determined not to let anything happen to my brother, Toby, or myself. During the coming months and then years, I would watch over him like a hawk. I wasn't going to let anyone harm him, especially not as long as I was around to guard him. All my life I had tried to protect my sisters and brothers from the clutches of Willie, Raymond and Jerry. It was as if they were devils to me. I felt men were never to be trusted again as long as I lived

I realized, as I grew older that what they had done to me was wrong. I vowed never to allow this to happen to my sisters and brothers, but who could I talk to about this? Who wouldn't just blame me for what had been done to me?

By having to leave, I was being pushed into a situation that I had no control over again. How was I supposed to just forget about my brothers and sisters? I knew they were too small to remember me. I knew it wouldn't be long and they would soon forget they had a sister. I was older and had been accustomed to taking care of them. Knowing I would never forget being like a mother to any of them, I tried to just hold onto the memories.

I was always crying on the inside and not on the outside, the tears flowing deep down within my soul. I was determined not to let anyone get too close to me. I had learned the hard way to not let anyone get close or they would try to harm me. "Never trust anyone but yourself and the good Lord up above," became my motto. Each day I prayed to God that he keep me in his arms until I met my mom in heaven.

The day I arrived at my father's home in Indianapolis my stomach was in knots. His wife, my new stepmother, DeAnn, greeted us by saying, "You are your father's children." She was letting us know that for that reason alone she was taking us into her home to raise us with her two children (later to be three children). DeAnn felt she was doing us a really big favor—a favor I could have lived without....

This greeting didn't sit well with me. I told her, "Lady, I knew who my real mother was and you are definitely not her." I also told her that I would never call her mom, and that she didn't need to feel obligated to do me any special favors. All the while I was crying inside.

I knew how to be hard and to play the tough game, because that is how I had played it for so many years. Cussing people out had become my way of protecting myself, and I was good at getting back at anyone who made me feel bad. Feeling lost and all alone without any control, I had to keep up a strong front. I was forced into a situation where a child's wishes just didn't count for very much. Since I was a minor, I had no rights. I was only eleven years old at the time. I was in dire need of a reality check, but who was be there to explain things to me?

Who could I tell that I didn't feel as though I was a child? I had grown up so fast without a childhood, I felt as if I was at least eighteen years old. I had never known what it felt like to just be a child, able to do childhood things like playing in the sand, making mud pies or just have fun out in the dirt. I felt I never had enough time to be loved and cared for by a mother.

The desire to have someone hold me and tell me that they loved me was screaming deep down in my soul, but I was too tough to say so. And, I really wasn't going to let DeAnn break me. Sometimes we just need to feel loved.

Knowing DeAnn was not going to be a real mom to me by her attitude, I had to keep up the charade. I never really acted like I cared much for her because she was so wicked-minded. She would find a reason to beat me daily. In fact, not many days went by that I didn't receive a beating. I really didn't hate DeAnn, I just wanted her to love me. Still I had learned not to let my guard down or I felt she would surely have hurt me badly. I didn't like her and she didn't care much for me—our feelings for each other were mutual.

The battle began as soon as I woke up in the morning. I would have to wake everyone in the house up, so those who needed to go to school could get ready as the other ones got ready for work. It was as though I had a built-in alarm clock within my mind. My stepmother would give me a time she needed to be out of bed, and for some strange reason I would say to myself, "I must be up at this time," and I was. Really, it was the only thing that I did that impressed DeAnn. This made me feel good, but it would only last for a few minutes, because when she really woke up she would start with the name-calling. She would treat me as though I was dirt.

I never really understood all the anger she had, and why it always seemed to be directed toward me. I had a lot of anger built up inside of me, too, for losing my mother at such a young age. One would think DeAnn would have understood my feelings. Instead, she'd say, "You remind me of your mother," to hurt me. I wondered why she blamed me for something I had no control over.

Ironically, I loved the fact that I looked like my mother. When I looked into the mirror, I would imagine what my mother really looked like. This was a source of comfort to me: An inner peace within my mind that no one could steal.

When I arrived home from school I had to clean the entire house. This didn't bother me, because I loved things to be neat (which is why I am a neat-freak even today). My stepmother saw this chore as an act of punishment. Little did she know that I really took pleasure in doing chores. I never bothered to share this with her, because I knew she would find a way to rob me of that pleasure as well.

The first thing I did was scrub all the walls with Spic 'n' Span, a cleanser-like laundry soap. Then I mopped the floors, cleaned the bathroom and swept the carpet. I would do the dishes, all the while she called me every bad name she could think of.

She would say things with no remorse like, "I was just a nappy-headed, little long-necked bitch." Oh, I will never forget those horrible words. She'd say to me, "You aren't good for anything. Just a total waste to society." And, "You are a freak of nature." I would just bite my tongue and swallow what little pride I had left.

Many times when my father was around, she'd say I didn't do anything to help keep the house clean, and then it was his turn to beat me as well. I remember there were times when I would have just finished cleaning the whole house and my stepmother would start her belittling and name-calling when she heard my father pull up into the driveway. She'd say, "You long-necked, nappy-headed little bitch. You don't do anything but sit on your lazy ass all day while I clean house." What a lying old witch, I would think to myself. My father would come into the house cussing at me about how I should have been working around the house to help her out. I knew this was DeAnn's way of protecting her own fat, lazy ass. That way my father wouldn't get angry with her for being in bed all day long.

My father asked DeAnn why she was always swearing at me when he came into the house. She would say, "Lenny, that child of yours never does shit to help me keep this house clean and I am tired of cleaning up after your kids." He would just take her at her word and commence to beat me. I never bothered to try and tell him that she was a liar, because I knew he wouldn't believe me. I just took his beatings and never looked back.

Her daughter, Trudy, whom she treated extremely well, got everything nicer than myself. She had new clothes and got gifts for any reason. She was a well-groomed girl. I often desired to have beautiful hair like hers and I felt ugly next to her.

Toby and I would have been grateful if DeAnn would have spent half the money my father gave her for us, instead of spending it on something for Trudy. Didn't DeAnn realize that we just wanted to be loved and treated like people, too? We were humans with emotions.

DeAnn was a mother who didn't want to take care of some other man's children, and yet she was forced to take us in. Even if a child is not your own and you are given this responsibility because of a marriage, you should treat that child as your own. Loving another man's child isn't a crime. And how can any adult hold a child accountable for looking like his or her mother? It wasn't like I had any control over that fact. The crime is committed when that child is abused, which is what DeAnn chose to do.

I just wanted DeAnn to understand that it wasn't easy for me to lose my mother at such a young age. Life was never the same for me after her death. I was devastated when it happened and found it difficult to accept her death. I had so many unanswered questions and my soul cried out for a little love.

There were times when I tried to tell my stepmother about the molestation problems I had endured while in Tennessee. She had no time to hear what I had to say, or maybe she just didn't care to hear my cries for affection. She may have been too battered by my father herself to feel anything about my concerns.

As time went on my soul cried out for someone to love me. My father worked all of the time, and when he wasn't working he was at the bar chasing after other women.

I found the church to be my source of comfort. Every Sunday I would get all dressed up and go to church. Church made me feel special and pretty, because I was dressed up and everyone was so nice to me. At the church I had a place of refuge, where different types of people came together and acted as one body.

After my mom died, I promised myself that I would be the best person I could be: never tell lies, always be willing to help, and try to get along with everyone, so I could get to heaven one day because I knew that is where I would find her. I promised myself that when I grew up and was fortunate enough to have children, I would love them forever and wouldn't beat or abuse them in any way—at least not the way my stepmother had abused me most of my young life.

I often wondered what could have happened to my stepmother to make her so angry inside. Whatever it was, it surely had to have been horrible. I often thought that when people were as evil as she was, they'd have to be born that way. As time went on, I realized that for anyone to be that angry, it had to be acquired over time.

I never had the chance to attend school much as a child growing up in Tennessee. I had to stay home and take care of my younger sisters and brothers. As time passed, I had convinced myself that I didn't mind and that this is how I showed by brothers and sisters what real love for someone was all about.

While I was in Indianapolis, my father and stepmother found out that I had never been to school. By this time I was twelve years old. I couldn't go to school when I was a child because nobody else would have been there to help with my little brothers and sisters, some who were not old enough to go to school yet. The school authorities told my stepmother I would have to be tested to see if I could be in a class with children my age or be placed in a class with younger students. I was fortunate that while in Tennessee my older stepsister taught me what she was learning in school. I would practice doing her schoolwork all day and evening. By the time everyone was home from the fields, I knew more than she had learned. I was blessed with the ability to comprehend a lot of schoolwork. My self-learning paid off; I was placed in class with kids my own age.

I knew my brother, Toby, wouldn't be able to keep up with the kids in his class, even though he had gone to school while in Tennessee. He never liked being in school because it difficult for him to learn. Toby was sort of quiet and didn't talk to anyone very much, so he was afraid to tell the teacher he didn't understand the schoolwork. In Indiana, Toby couldn't be put in class with kids his own age. He was put back a grade level. Toby and I were very close. We felt we only had each other to depend upon, so we took care of each other.

I cried when I was sick, never wanting to miss going to school. I craved knowledge and was driven to achieve. While in school I began to excel in English, science, social studies and biology. Math was always hard for me. Although I passed it with B's and C's, I never liked it at all.

I felt safer at school than being at home with DeAnn. At school, I got into sports and became an avid runner. Back in Tennessee I could run like the wind—often faster than my brothers—because running had become a way of escaping their abuse. They couldn't have their way with me if they couldn't catch me. There were times though, that I welcomed their sick attention, because I felt it was better than no attention at all. While attending school in Indianapolis, I enjoyed participating in all sports, and particularly loved the balance beam in gymnastics.

At twelve, I got my first job as babysitter for my minister, Mr. Williams. His two children were unruly and hard to manage, but I had fun playing games and reading to them. Just being their friend was all right with me. I had always loved children and already knew that someday I wanted to have kids of my own. I usually bought school supplies with the money I made.

My minister was a kind, generous and patient person. It was comical how he chased his children around, trying to get them to do things. Here is a man who had all these great qualities as the leader of his church, but he couldn't get his own kids to mind him.

Mr. Williams had a dark side, too. It's amazing how we tend to believe that people in such a position as a minister are supposed to be perfect and without sin. There seems to be good and bad in every race and profession.

I told myself that God would punish Mr. Williams for chasing after the young girls and pretending to be such a true Christian. He was a married man and should have known better than to chase after young girls. Unfortunately, one day while Mr. Williams was cruising in his new, shiny black Cadillac, he had a car accident and he was found decapitated. What a shame that this happened to Mr. Williams, I thought.

By the time I was fourteen years old, I was tired of asking my father for a dollar and explaining what I was going to do with it. I decided I needed a new job and I put in applications at several different places after school one day. About a week later, the manager of Happy Chicken called me in for an interview. The interview went well and I landed my first real job. After my first paycheck, compared to my babysitting pay I was bringing in big bucks. I was making eighty dollars a week. Each week I would buy myself two new dresses. I really thought I had it made.

Then one day DeAnn came into my room, opened my closet and took out some of my new dresses. She then gave several of them to my stepsister. She told Trudy I never wore them because I had too many clothes to be able to wear them all. I told DeAnn I hadn't worn those dresses yet because I was saving them for a special occasion. She told me to shut up. I did as she asked, knowing the consequences if I didn't.

Later that day I was still angry and I said to DeAnn, "Lady, you are fat, and your daughter will be fat someday." When I said this I felt so strong and I believed no matter what she did to me it would have been worth it. She laughed and said I didn't know what I was talking about.

As she left my room I called her a big, fat-assed old bitch. When she heard this she came back into my room, reached into my closet and grabbed my favorite, beautiful red dress. I told her I would tell my father if she didn't give it back to me. She told me she would beat the shit out of me if I told him.

"Then you'll just have to do it, because I am telling him and I am tired of you taking my clothes," I said. DeAnn turned around and hit me hard, but I repeated that I would tell my father. She finally decided to give me back my red dress and left my room. DeAnn knew that I was stubborn and didn't mind taking a "whipping" from time to time because I had grown accustomed to them.

When I was in high school I was known for wearing wigs, because my stepmother refused to do my hair even though she was a licensed beautician. She never had a problem doing her daughter Trudy's hair. She had beautiful, long, black, wavy hair. As for me, I just had a head full of nappy, short and kinky hair.

One day I told DeAnn I would like her to do my hair, so I didn't have to wear an ugly wig. I wanted to feel pretty like Trudy. DeAnn said my hair would look the same no matter what she did to it and I would still be a little, ugly, long-necked bitch. DeAnn was right there at home with all the tools and skills as a beautician. At the age I was, I could have afforded to pay for my hair myself, but I didn't believe that I should have to spend my little money on a beautician to get my hair done at a salon when DeAnn could have helped me.

I told her that when I was a little girl my mother dressed me up as a boy and my brother as a girl, because he had long, black hair that was pretty like Trudy's. My mother used to dress me like a boy, brogan shoes and all, while my brother wore dresses. He had a head full of long, black, curly hair and he looked so beautiful. My hair was just the opposite: kinky and nappy. I believed my brother looked better than I did, too. Then one day my Uncle Rudy came to visit us and he took my brother Toby into town for a haircut. When my mother came home she was so devastated that she cried for hours looking at Toby without all of his long black hair. At that very moment, I remembered feeling like a girl for the first time and what a joy it was.

For some reason, on this particular day I really wanted DeAnn to do my hair, so I could look beautiful just like Trudy. DeAnn looked at me and grinned and said she would give it some thought. She said that I was too ugly for it to make a real difference, no matter how she did my hair. It wasn't the hair that was my problem, she said, it was my looks. She wouldn't do my hair that day. DeAnn finally decided to do my hair and it turned out very nice. It made me wonder why she couldn't have done it sooner rather than later.

When my friends came over after school, she talked about me like a dog. They would tell her they were ashamed of the way she talked to me and how she put me down. They told her that it wasn't normal for a mother to do that to her child. She told them she wasn't my mother, but my stepmother.

While staying with DeAnn I learned how evil some people could be. This woman made it her business to ridicule me most of my waking hours spent at home. It was as though she had nothing better to amuse herself with. She never went anywhere, instead always lying around the house, sleeping most of the time and gaining weight. She weighed almost 400 pounds.

When I was younger, I used to think that one day I would look like DeAnn. My friends reminded me that she wasn't my real mother. They asked me if my real mother was fat. I told them that she was small. My friends said I would be just like her. This made me very happy.

When she didn't have anything amusing to watch on TV, she would beat me just for something to do. When DeAnn beat me, she beat me so badly that I would bleed from the licks of the belt. It left welts all over my back and legs.

She also liked skinning and braiding three small branches together, so they could dig real deep into my flesh. DeAnn told me that if the branches I brought to her were too small, then she would have to braid several of them together. Most times I tried to bring her a medium-sized branch. But the medium-sized branch I brought never seemed big enough—at least not in her eyes.

Everything seemed larger than it really was for me in her world. When she was ready to beat me I was told to go strip off all of my clothes and lay over the bathtub naked so she could make sure I felt every lick. Sometimes as I lay there waiting for her to come and give me my punishment, it seemed like I was lying there for hours just waiting to be beaten. So why didn't I just get up from there and run away at least far enough away to cry for help? I didn't get up and leave because DeAnn had instilled such fear in us kids about running away that it never crossed my mind to leave.

One day she beat me so bad that I became too angry to cry. She said, "You had better cry, you little bitch, or I will beat your ass until you are beyond bloody." I pretended to cry just to please her, because this seemed to quell her urgency to beat me. She seemed to get a sick pleasure out of seeing me tormented.

By the time I was sixteen years old, I was still an adventurous child who liked doing what the guys did most of the time. At times when my brother and I were outside playing with our friends, the other boys would pick on Toby and I would beat them up. I believed no one had a right to pick on my brother. I felt I had to protect him from all harm. Toby would run away from the boys screaming. I would run after him and try to get him to fight back. If they beat him up, I retaliated. When he wouldn't fight for himself, I would fight the tormentors. I tried to get Toby to stand up for himself. I was bound and determined he wouldn't be a wimp. A boy can never become a real man unless he learns to fight back.

4

Not by Choice

My stepmother told me that I wasn't your normal sixteen-year-old girl. I had very small breasts and I acted like one of the guys. She said this wasn't normal behavior for a young lady to portray. This would make me angrier. So angry, in fact, that eventually someone would have to pay ...

How was I to know what normal behavior was? I had never had anything resembling normal in my life before. The rebel independent in me didn't want to please this overbearing and abusive woman.

Near the end of my sixteenth year, I asked my stepmother for her permission to get birth control pills. She told me that I had better not have sex with anyone or she would kill me herself. I said I hadn't had sex yet, but that I might try it one day to please my boyfriend so he'd desire me over the other girls he was flirting with.

At this time, sex meant nothing to me, because I had such bad experiences when I was very young. How could sex mean anything to me when I always associated it with something ugly or shameful? I had never learned to trust men since my childhood. The only time I believed in my heart I would ever think about having sex would be when I got married.

DeAnn refused to give me the pill, but she put her daughter on it at the age of fourteen. She claimed that Trudy was different … she had more sense than I did.

My boyfriend, Tony, had been pressuring me to having sex with him. When I told him I wasn't ready to have sex with him or anyone else because I was too young, he had sex with other girls from the neighborhood. I told myself I didn't care who he had sex with—as long as it wasn't me. I was afraid of having sex because I knew it would probably hurt me. The thought of sex made me sick to my stomach. It had become too horrifying for me to even imagine what it would feel like. I wanted to wait until after I was married to have sex again.

One evening I attended Tony's sister's baby shower. It was a nice gathering and there were lots of games and gifts to win and other fun things to do. After the shower, Tony and I went downstairs to listen to music. We began hugging and kissing. I felt comfortable with him caressing me until I felt he was getting out of control. I asked him to stop what he was doing. He refused, using the excuse that he was so excited because I was turning him on. I tried to fight him off, but found that he was too strong for me to handle. He began to rip my clothes as he tried to take them off. Finally, he ripped the zipper right out of my pants.

I screamed for help. No one heard me. No one came to help me. Tony climbed on top of me and forced himself inside of me. It hurt so badly that I thought I would just die. I kept fighting and struggling to get away, but he was so big and strong. All of a sudden, his brother Joe appeared and tried to make him get off of me. He and Tony began to fight, but it was too late to help me, Tony had already ejaculated inside of me.

I thought to myself, "What am I to do?" I couldn't talk to my stepmother about this incident when I got home, because she would just say I was just being fresh and that I got what I deserved. I thought that she would probably beat me and I didn't feel like being beaten anymore. I was tired enough already from the struggle with Tony.

When I arrived at home, DeAnn was sitting in the living room watching television and eating, as usual. She looked at me and asked how the shower had gone. I said that Tony's sister had received a lot of nice things. As I walked past her, she asked me what had happened to my pants. I told her that my zipper had broken, said goodnight and went to my room.

As time went on, it never dawned on me that I might be pregnant from this one incident. I had always thought that it took a long time for someone to get pregnant and you had to "make love" to get pregnant. It was silly of me to even think this way, but it shows how little I knew about sexual relations. As time passed, I became less and less active, but still didn't know what was wrong with me. I had been a young lady who always went outside as soon as I got home from school. Not any more. I had no energy at all; I just wanted to go to sleep.

One day when I came home from school, my stepmother was waiting for me by the front door. She told me to head straight to the bathroom. I did as she asked, not knowing what to expect. She told me to take off my blouse and turn around and face her. When I had done as she asked, she took the nipple of my breast into her hand and squeezed it hard. It hurt so much. She slapped me across my face and called me a slut. Then she told me that I was pregnant.

"I am not a slut," I said, "and I didn't even have sex willingly. Tony forced himself on me." He had raped me and I finally had enough nerve to inform her of this.

I told her I didn't think that I could get pregnant because I was forced to have sex and I wasn't a willing participant. DeAnn said that she knew I was stupid, but not that stupid. She then proceeded to call me degrading names.

I could tell by the look on her face that she didn't believe that I hadn't wanted to have sex with Tony and that it had been forced on me. She had always needed to believe the worst in me, and now she would have a legitimate reason for whipping me. She said I was just too fast and needed to be taught a lesson. She beat me when she first found out, but quit beating me after that. She would slap me across my face from time to time.

As more time elapsed, DeAnn came up with the idea that she would make me put the baby up for adoption. I told her that I wouldn't do that or have an abortion.

I felt that I had let this happen. I felt that my life was over as I knew it, and that I would never get to join the Army, which I had planned to do when I graduated. I was determined not to have an abortion. I was willing to be responsible for my own actions. Deep down inside I knew the baby would be someone who would love me. It made me feel special.

DeAnn threatened to put me into a maternity home for unwed mothers. She kept her promise, but not before scaring the living daylights out of me. One day she told me to sit down and told me how excruciating the pain was going to be when I had my child.

Sometimes women died during childbirth, DeAnn said, and I should really consider ending the pregnancy before it was too late. Her aim was to frighten me—and she sure did. As usual, I began to believe everything that DeAnn was saying to me about having a child. My mind was filled with doubts about whether I should go through with having it. I thought I might die for real, because I had heard that sometimes when a doctor put a patient to sleep they never woke up, but each day I told myself the Lord would take care of me, because he always took care of babies and fools. I didn't believe he was going to let me die.

Upon arriving at the home for unwed teenage mothers, I felt a sigh of relief. The mother of the house seemed nice and friendly. There were other girls my age living there and all of them were very friendly to me and made me feel welcome. We were like one big, happy family. Each of us was assigned daily chores. I couldn't believe I didn't have to do all the chores myself. When I was at home with DeAnn, I had to do all the chores. Some of the girls prepared lunch and some dinner or supper, but we took turns. We shared the laundry duties.

We took parenting classes to help bring up our babies the right way. There were no restrictions on what we did in our spare time, but we weren't allowed to go out partying or anything like that.

Back at my high school, I was on the graduating list. I went to the school to be measured for my cap and gown. My stepmother had allowed me take some of the money I had saved from working to buy my class ring for graduation. What she had forgotten to mention was that she had no intention of allowing me to walk across the stage with the other students. To her, it was a privilege to do that and I had lost the privilege when I became pregnant. There was no way she was going to allow me up on that stage in my condition to embarrass her. What did she have to be embarrassed about?

I wasn't showing anyway. No one would have know I was pregnant if I hadn't confided in my home economics teacher. DeAnn knew when she let me buy my cap and gown that she would never allow me to walk across that stage. I bought a cap and gown that were never worn. I was so sad that she wouldn't let me receive my diploma at the ceremony, but such was life.

While staying at the maternity home, the housemother and I became very close. She was someone who took the time to listen to what had been locked up inside of me for so many years. She knew that I had a lot of pent-up frustrations within me that needed to be released. With her I was able to vent and get rid of a lot of the anger, hurt and pain that I was feeling inside.

One morning, Linda and Annie (two other girls in the home) were going into town to do some shopping and I wanted to go with them. The housemother didn't want me to go with them. She said she had a bad feeling about the trip and that I should stay behind with her. Linda hadn't had her license very long, but I trusted her driving so I went along for the ride. About a mile and a half down the road, a drunk driver ran a red light, wrecking our car so bad we had to crawl out the window.

I was about eight months pregnant at the time. In the ambulance on the way to the hospital, I told the ambulance driver I felt like I had to urinate. This made the driver think that I was going into labor and he sped up. He didn't want me to have my baby in the ambulance. I asked the driver to please slow down, because he was scaring me.

DeAnn had told me that labor was really horrible and the pain would be unbearable. At the time, my pain didn't feel severe, so I knew I wasn't in labor. I just needed to go to the restroom, because the accident had scared me so badly.

My neck was hurting and my legs were filed with chips of glass. After arriving at the hospital, the doctors decided that I was too close to having my baby for them to give me any medication for the pain. The doctor had to pick the glass out of my legs without any medication, which was uncomfortable but I was able to bear it. I had to wear a neck brace, but I was able to leave the hospital.

I was not unfamiliar with the agony of pain, because DeAnn had hardened me up inside and it was a part of my daily nourishment while living at home with her. After the accident, DeAnn came to the maternity home and brought me back home with her.

As part of my recovery, I went to physical therapy. DeAnn sued the man who caused the accident. The money was put into a trust until I turned twenty-one years old, when DeAnn had my stepsister forge my name on the documents and took the money.

The mother of the maternity house knew my situation at home would probably not get any better, and she didn't want me to leave. I missed being at home with my brother, so I left the maternity home and went home with DeAnn.

I believed that my being away might have given DeAnn a chance to leave her anger towards me in the past. This was too much to wish for, because when I got home she was still as evil as ever. I should have known better than to wish for something that would never be.

One afternoon DeAnn asked me if I had decided whether to give my baby up yet. I told her she already knew what my decision was before I went to the maternity home. My mind hadn't changed all of a sudden. She then informed me that she had set up a court date and that I was to appear before a judge in the morning to give up the baby for adoption.

In the courtroom, the judge discovered that I would be eighteen years old before my baby was due to be born and threw the case out of court. DeAnn couldn't believe she had no control over this matter, especially when she had controlled my life for the past seven years. This didn't make her very happy with me at all, but for me at long last I had won the battle and the right to make my own decisions.

The delivery was nothing like DeAnn told me it was going to be. I was so scared when I was going to have the baby. I dreaded the day that I was supposed to deliver. It was actually a beautiful experience. It wasn't a difficult labor or delivery. I was happy to have my baby girl, because it made me feel like that now I had someone who would finally love me back. I was determined that I would never let anything happen to my baby, because I was going to protect her. Shanita was so beautiful. My stepmother had been telling me that my child would be ugly, and while I was pregnant I believed her, but when she was born I knew she was wrong.

DeAnn asked me to let my three-year-old sister, Kelly, hold Shanita. When I refused DeAnn's command, I knew once and for all that it was time for me to move on.

One afternoon when Shanita was about three months old, DeAnn sent me along with my sister, Kelly, to the store. She watched us walk down the street toward the store. I had Kelly by the hand as I led her down the sidewalk. Suddenly, the sidewalk had an uprising in it and Kelly tripped and fell. My stepmother called me back to the house and slapped me across the face. It brought tears to my eyes while Kelly tried to tell her that I wasn't the cause of her falling down. DeAnn refused to listen to Kelly's cries.

I had dealt with her abuse enough and I knew it was time for me to leave, so that afternoon I packed up Shanita and my things and moved down the street to live with my boyfriend and his family. Even though Tony had raped me, I knew it would be much safer living with him than continuing to live with DeAnn. Also, I was from Tennessee where women just didn't have children out of wedlock. It was considered a disgrace, and I didn't want Shanita teased for not having a father.

I was lucky to find a job close to home shortly after moving in with Tony and his family. Tony would drive me to work most afternoons. Sometimes another girl would sit between us when he drove me to work. He had no respect for his child or me, yet I tolerated his insulting behavior because it kept his icky hands off me.

At night when he picked me up from work I'd ask him how he could do the things he did. He said he thought he was just a fine example of a man, especially when I was the one refusing to satisfy his sexual needs. He told me I was the one he truly loved, so it shouldn't matter that he was just using those women for sex.

Worst thing is, I believed him. Tony said most other girls would be happy to be his girlfriend and that should be good enough to satisfy me as well.

I tried to push back the pain I felt deep down inside and swallow what pride I had, because at least I was away from my wicked stepmother. I had some peace of mind away from her abusive behavior.

Tony's mother told him that I was too dark-skinned for him to be serious about, even though we had a beautiful, bright-skinned daughter together. She wanted Tony to be with a light-skinned black girl with long, pretty hair. I didn't have the hair, nor was I light-skinned. Tony's mother was really color-struck. She wanted his chosen one to be light, bright and darn near white. What does a person's color have to do with the kind of individual he or she turns out to be, anyway?

Tony's stepfather, Derk, always treated me as though I was special. He made Tony get up early every morning to look for a job. Little did he know that after he went to work at the post office, Tony's mother would let him back into the house so he could go back to sleep. Then she would wonder why he didn't go out and look for a job on his own once he was up. She thought his stepfather was just being too hard on poor little Tony. I believe this is why Tony is still lazy to this very day. He thinks a man's only responsibility is to have children and then run off with some other woman who didn't have any.

At times Tony and I would argue over his wandering ways. I hoped that trying to talk about it would change him. All the talking never worked, because he was lazy and never wanted much more than a roof over his head and food to put in his mouth.

One day, Tony's great aunt from Minnesota came down to visit his mother. Aunt Carrie was a very tall, dark-skinned lady who seemed special to me right from the start. She and I talked a lot as I told her about the environment I had grown up in. I told her a lot of things that a person would normally only tell someone they had known for years.

Before she left, she told me that if I ever wanted to come to Minnesota, I was more than welcome to live with her. Auntie said she thought I should leave her no-good nephew and give her state a try. She left me her phone number and told me to call her anytime I needed to talk.

5

Northward Bound

About a month later, I asked Aunt Carrie if I could come to Minnesota and try and start a new life for my daughter and myself. Auntie said we could stay with her to get our lives started. I told her that my things were already packed and I was ready to hop on a plane to make Minnesota my new home.

Suddenly, Tony felt it was time for him to be a responsible father to our daughter and decided to drive me to Minnesota, so we could start a new life together. I was so darn stupid. I wanted a name for Shanita, so my being an unmarried mother and her a girl without a father wouldn't embarrass either of us. As a mother, I believed it was my responsibility to protect Shanita at all costs. Being as naive as I was, I had believed DeAnn when she told me no one would want to raise another man's child. DeAnn had made it obvious that she unhappy when Toby and I came to live with them.

We arrived in Minnesota in January 1972. I remember how unbelievably cold it was. I thought I was in Alaska. I wondered if I could ever adapt to the cold. I had wanted to go to Minnesota and start a new life, but never in my wildest dreams would I have believed it could be so cold. I hated cold weather and always wanted to live somewhere where it was warm, like Tennessee or Arizona. During my first few weeks in Minnesota, I didn't have any real winter clothing, but I learned very quickly to get them.

It was luck that helped me land my first job in the Twin Cities at a plastic injection molding company. I had never done this kind of work. I was taught to run an injection-molding machine, making all kind of different plastic parts. I had a good attitude and was willing to learn how to do a good job. My boss said I appeared to be a highly motivated person and he liked that in an individual. I loved to work. It made me feel very proud of my accomplishments.

Every day I worked hard and never missed a day. Tony didn't have a job yet. He just lounged around the house all day. Because my life had been so bad with my stepmother, my situation with Tony wasn't abusive enough for me to want to leave his no-good self. Dump him for what, I wondered, another asshole worse than him?

Tony never graduated from high school. He always fell asleep during class. He had been a lazy person most of his life, and he saw no reason to want to try and change just yet.

Every day upon arriving home from work, Tony expected me to get right into the kitchen and start making his supper. I couldn't believe this man's attitude, so bold and demanding. It was as though I had become his servant and keeper. As the months passed by, I was getting tired of working all of the time and Tony doing nothing. When I started complaining about his bad ways, he decided it was time for him to start running the streets. Auntie had told me that I needed to watch him, because women in Minnesota sometimes took care of men just to have one. I told her I couldn't work all day and think about what Tony was doing while I was working.

One evening I arrived home from work and cooked dinner. Tony wasn't at home, so I waited and waited for him. About midnight, Tony still wasn't home, so I went to bed. At about 2:00 a.m. he arrived home smelling of alcohol and perfume.

After asking him where he had been, he slapped me across my face so hard tears filled my eyes. I told him if he ever slapped me again, I would leave his no-good ass. He said he was so sorry that he had slapped me, and told me it would never happen again. Afterwards, we kissed and we made up.

As the months wore on, Tony's behavior became worse. He was staying out longer than usual and he shared with me a lot of the things he was doing with other women. It was as though he got off on sharing his illicit affairs with me. I didn't believe him when he said that he was trying to get a job or stop chasing women.

There were times I would catch him red-handed with one slut or another. We would be at a party together, and he'd force me to take a few hits on a joint so I would pass out (pot made me so sleepy). While I was passed out, he would be hanging all over some other woman. There were times I would wake up and catch him in a corner with a woman he had met at the party. He just didn't seem to care much anymore about whether he was caught messing around or not.

Tony began to smoke more and more weed. He said he wanted to buy weed and sell some for extra money. I told him that our baby couldn't live off of weed and if he sold it he would be breaking the law. It didn't matter what I said, he still smoked away our grocery money.

Tony turned into such a pothead. What a laugh he was at times. A waste to society, I thought. Never wanting to make him feel less than a man, I tried to keep my mouth shut, but not when it came to taking food out of the mouths of my children. By this time, I had given birth to our second child, Teddie, so we now had a son, as well.

One day Aunt Carrie told us we had been living with her long enough, almost three years. She said it was time for Tony to give his children a name and marry me. Tony told Auntie that he wanted to marry me, but I said I didn't want to marry an asshole like him. Aunt Carrie told me to marry him if, for nothing else, to give the children their father's name. We decided to get married and to have a small church wedding. I phoned my stepmother and brother in Indianapolis to tell them of our plans. They surprised me by deciding to come up for the wedding. I didn't think my step mom would feel it was important enough to come up for my wedding, but she flew in with my brother. This was a pivotal point in our relationship. After this, I think she began to really believe I loved Tony. She was nice to me for a change at the wedding.

The night after our wedding, Tony took my own shoe and beat me with it. He told me that now he owned me and I was his property. He also told me that if I ever threatened to leave him again, he would "beat the living shit out of me." Tony also informed me that if I ever swore at him again, he would beat me.

Tony was going over daily to his friend's house to play cards. He played cards all night long and wouldn't come home until the following morning. This kind of behavior became sickening to me. He was acting like a single man gone crazy and astray.

What a jerk I had chosen for a husband. You never really know a man—or a woman—until you marry him or her. Sometimes they can be as different as night and day. I wondered how long I could tolerate his behavior. When I went along and got tired of playing cards with Tony and his friend, I would tell him that I had played cards long enough. He would tell me to go on home and lie down and that he would meet me there later.

Many times I found myself waiting up for hours for him. Many times he wouldn't come home until the following morning. Once when he came home, he told me he had slept with a girl named Angie. He said she was so ugly and looked like a goat, but he didn't care, she had an ass. When he told me his exploits, I cried my heart out. He loved making up with me. It was more romantic to him. Because sex was a release for me after all of the emotion and drama, our sex together was less inhibited and stressed. This kind of lovemaking really turned him on.

Tony would have sex with anyone willing to give it to him, and he never seemed to get enough. He gave me crabs twice and gonorrhea twice. For the gonorrhea, I had to have two shots of penicillin in my rear. The second time Tony gave me gonorrhea, I believed him when he told me the reason he had a scab on his penis was because he had zipped his penis in his pant zipper. Like a fool, I believed him. To keep me from leaving, Tony would tell me that no one else would want me and that no man would want a woman who already had two kids. Growing up like I did in an abusive home, I believed him.

One evening as I was lying on the couch watching TV, my stomach started cramping and the pain was so excruciating that I couldn't pull myself up from the couch. I told Tony I thought I was having an appendicitis, so he picked me up, carried me out to the car and drove me to the hospital.

After the doctor finished with my examination, he said I had to be hospitalized because I had an inflamed pelvis. He said the infection had been caused by the gonorrhea my husband had given me, once again. The infection had spread around my liver.

The doctor said he wouldn't release me after treatment until he spoke privately with my husband. After the doctor was finished talking to Tony, he spoke to us together. He told Tony that I should leave him, and that he should be ashamed of himself for all the things he had put me through. Before he left the room, two guards came and escorted my husband into a room where he was administered treatment. And who had to hold his head to her chest to console him like he was a child? Me, his loving wife (the Idiot …). You would have thought this would've been enough for me to leave him, but I gave him another chance.

After we arrived back home, I refused to speak to Tony for hours as he tried to explain why he was so late in telling me. I didn't want to hear it. He said sometimes women wanted him to have sex with them so bad that he just had to "service them," because he didn't know what else to do. He certainly wasn't going to say no to some free ass. He said he knew he was a dog. I felt sorry for him and wanted to comfort him and make him feel better, so I decided to give in to his sexual cravings and have sex with him.

At that time, I still didn't understand why sex didn't mean anything to me. I felt I had to moan and groan as though I was having an orgasm, when really I felt nothing. There were times I truly thought that I must be messed up because I couldn't get into feeling anything when he made love to me. When Tony wanted to have oral sex, I was really turned off. At the time, I felt as though it was not natural.

It was disgusting for me to have sex with Tony because he would slobber all over me. I didn't want to have sex with him, because I wasn't free and relaxed. If you love sex, you want it—I hated sex. I didn't get anything out of it. I didn't realize then what I was saying when I told him that if he wanted sex like that he would have to find it somewhere else.

After I told Aunt Carrie what the doctor said about my gonorrhea, she said I should leave her no-good nephew. I told her that I was still in love with him and I wanted to be with him. Since I had never had much love, I hungered for it and anytime anyone showed affection towards me, I believed it was the real thing. I craved attention and whenever Tony was around, he gave it to us. It seemed like he really did adore his children and I.

One weekend Tony's mother came to Minnesota for one of her many trips. She always got drunk and cursed me out for no apparent reason. I hadn't disrespected her, because if nothing else, she was my elder. I had always been taught to respect my elders, no matter how disrespectful they might be to me.

Tony's mother would tell me that I was wrong for her son. How wrong could she have been? She hurt me so much talking like this. I would take all of her put-downs because she was Tony's mother. Some adults don't deserve respect, and she was one of those adults, but I gave it to her anyway. I always tried to be a good person, to love my neighbor and to be humble—even when they are disrespectful to me.

One night, Aunt Carrie had more than she could take of Tony's mom's bad attitude. She came into the kitchen and told her not to swear at me anymore or she would have to leave. Auntie told Tony's mother to listen to her for a change. She told her that her son was the asshole and that I had taken so much crap off of him that it was unbelievable. She said that if she were I, she would have left Tony a long time ago and so would Tony's mom.

Aunt Carrie told her that her son was worthless and not worth my time. She told Tony's mom to get the hell out of her house and not to come back. Tony's mom was very angry with me for Aunt Carrie's attitude toward her, but I was proud of Auntie for standing up to her, because I never could.

She was right. Tony never brought any money home to the kids and me. He smoked all of his paycheck away. I worked all day, came home and fixed supper for him and the kids. There were times when I worked daily labor during the evening hours just to keep up with all the bills. Why? Because his money was being spent on all the sluts he could impress, while I waited on him to come home at night.

Through all this, my kids and I were very close. I would never let Tony put his hands on the children. He knew I wouldn't ever let him treat our kids in an abusive way. Conversely, anytime anyone said something loud to me or was mean to me, my children would run to me to protect me.

One summer after working for the plastics company for about two years, I was tired of working there and I decided to apply for another type of job, so I went to an electronics company that made computer components. I had never done this type of work before, but the company manager was impressed with my previous work history so he decided to give me a chance.

After learning how to strip the wires for the terminals, I learned how to solder the computer terminals onto the computer membranes. This procedure required a microscope to see well enough to get the wires straight on the terminals. I never seemed to quite get the technique of using the microscope, but I saw well enough that I didn't need a microscope. I had burned my fingers so many times trying to look through the scope instead of the terminal that my boss told me I didn't have to use the scope, because my work was good without it.

I worked for this company for about four years, when one day my husband's aunt's boyfriend passed away and I needed time off for the funeral. My boss stated that the boyfriend was not immediate family and I couldn't have the time off. I asked him how he could put a value on his life, he wasn't God.

Because of this incident, I decided to resign from the electronics company. I felt they were too uncaring. I had avoiding quitting my job, because I felt that it would look bad on my resume, but I resigned anyways. I applied for a secretarial position with a large insurance company. I had never worked as a secretary before, but I had enjoyed my high school business classes, so I decided to give it a try.

I interviewed with a man named Mr. Sherman. He said he was impressed with my application. He told me he wanted me to talk to two other department heads and, depending on the outcome of their ratings, he would let me know if I had the job.

He wanted to know what made me think I could do the job at hand. I told him the truth: I had taken typing in high school and had never typed over 35 words per minute, because I too busy watching my fingers as they moved across the keyboard. To my amazement, Mr. Sherman was still impressed by the fact that I had taken business and science classes and had never worked in a business-related field.

All three men who interviewed me said they were pleased with my abilities, as well as my attitude. They offered me the position. The job included on-the-job training classes. The on-the-job training instructor, Angela, was assigned to teach me English, math and typing skills as part of my work at the company. I was in class part of the day, and the rest of the day doing the actual work. After being in class for a week, Angela determined that I didn't need English any longer because I was already at college level. During typing class, Angela insisted that I stop watching my fingers because it was slowing down my typing speed. She told me that was why I never got over 35 words per minute while in high school.

I didn't listen to Angela about watching my fingers, so she put tape over all of the keys on my typewriter. I couldn't see what the keys said anymore, I only saw white tape. This made me angry and I lashed out at Angela. I told her she was a racist and that I didn't like her.

Lo and behold, three weeks after being in Angela's class, I really began to see a difference in my typing speed. My fingers were going across the keyboard at warp speed. She had taught me to type 90 words per minute without any mistakes and how to type so I wouldn't forget where the keys were.

No one had ever taken this kind of time to teach me anything. This lady earned my undying respect, and I wish I knew where she was today. Before I left her class, I realized she had taught me a valuable lesson: Never put limits on your achievements. She also showed me that I performed better than I felt I ever could. I learned to be hungry for knowledge, because knowledge will guide your path and be food for your dying soul.

While working for the electronics company I received merit raises every three months. My boss said I had received more merit raises than anyone had in his company's history.

I remember it was storming something terrible outside one day. I am afraid of lightning, so I told my boss I couldn't type my work while it was storming. He asked me why I couldn't. I told him because I believed the lightning might kill me. Instead of getting angry, he let me take a break whenever a storm brewed up.

While in Tennessee my stepbrother had locked me into a closet one day while it was storming outside. Usually during a storm, I would run through the house, screaming bloody murder, thinking that I would be struck by the lightning. That day as the storm was getting worse I was still locked in the closet. Soon I heard everyone running outside to the storm shelter, but I couldn't get out of the closet. When the storm was over, my mom heard me screaming from inside the closet. She opened the door and said that I looked petrified. I couldn't breathe. My mom whipped my stepbrother for locking me in the closet. To this day, I am terrified of lightning.

My relationship with Tony was going downhill fast. I finally wanted to get out of the relationship. One day we were driving down Lake Street, Tony was driving and our son and daughter were sitting between us. Tony's sister was in the back seat. I asked Tony why he had spent all the money on weed again. He became frustrated with my question, and I could see the rage building on his face. He always turned red as a beet when something or someone angered him, then his nostrils would start flaring.

I almost knew what was going to happen next. He reached across the kids and hit me hard across my face. Blood began squirting everywhere. He let go of the steering wheel to try and slap me again. His sister grabbed his arms and tried to restrain him. I asked her to let go of his arms before he ran into something and killed us all. What she didn't know is that I had been slapped many times by her brother and survived before. Most times when he hit me, I thought I must have had it coming for talking back to him. After being treated like this for so long, I had become immune to the physical abuse from my husband.

One evening when we were at home, Tony wanted to get out of the house, but I had wanted him to spend some time with the kids and I. Shanita was in the bathroom with me when Tony slapped me across my face and knocked me down onto the floor. He jumped on top of me and put his knee into my chest and told me he was going to cut my throat and then kill himself. He pulled a knife from his pants and put it to my throat. It wasn't until he said he wanted to die that I told him to kill himself first. The look on his face was so strange, I began to laugh. I couldn't stop laughing at this foolish man, as well as myself for being such an idiot.

He wouldn't budge, so I reached up and grabbed his bottom lip and tried to tear it off. He jumped up hollering that I had hurt his silly lip. I thought, so what. Was I supposed to just lie there and let him slit my throat and say, "Honey, thank you for the lesson." What a bully I was living with. A real living nightmare had come to life and I knew I had to get out sooner than later.

The following morning at work I asked my boss for a three-month medical leave of absence because of personal problems. I told him I needed some time off to get my head in order and find somewhere safe for my kids and myself. After approaching my boss, I wanted to take the medical leave so bad it felt as though I could taste my freedom. My boss denied letting me take a leave, because he said he needed me at work too much. I tried hard to continue working, but the stress was too much.

I went to see a doctor because I felt weak and drained most of the time. The doctor put me on Valium. I started out on 2.5 milligrams. Then I went to 5 milligrams and then up to 10 milligrams. I felt as though I didn't know whether I was coming or going most of the time. All I knew for sure was that was it and I couldn't take it anymore. I told the doctor I had enough. No more pills. I knew that when I would came down from the Valium, my problems were still there. It was time to quit covering up my problems and face them, or so I thought.

I wrote a letter of resignation and submitted it to my supervisor. He asked me to come into his office and told me he was willing to give me the three months medical leave of absence instead of losing me. But by the time he made this offer, I wasn't functioning well. I felt it was in his best interest, as well as mine, to resign. As I went for the door to leave, my boss could see the pain on my face, because I really loved him as a person and my job.

Before my last day, my boss let eight engineers off from work for a half a day to help move me out of our house while Tony was at work. By the time he got home, I was mostly moved out. The company also paid my rent for the next three months, and they took me grocery shopping to pick up enough stuff for my kids and I for at least the next three months. I think he believed that I would want to come back to work after being off for a while. Deep down inside I knew that I didn't have any intention of going back to work anytime soon.

As time went on, I needed money, so I decided to apply for unemployment. My former boss contested my unemployment, because he really wanted me to come back to work when I began to feel better. My unemployment judgment was decided in my favor, and I was rewarded an additional six weeks' benefits. The committee that awarded the employment benefits had realized that I had been hurt beyond repair, and that walking out on a man I believed I still loved had traumatized me.

There were so many times I didn't understand my own feelings. As many times as Tony had misused me and abused me physically, any normal person would have left him, but I never really felt I knew what was considered a normal relationship. As a child, all I remembered was watching my mother being abused by my stepfather, so it was "normal" for my man to beat me in my own sick mind.

My husband found out that I was filing for a divorce and he contested it. Tony was one angry individual. He was angry at life itself, because nothing seemed to be playing out like he had hoped. He believed that he owned me because we were married, and I would take whatever crap he gave me. What he didn't understand was that everyone (even me) gets tired of the abuse some day.

6

On My Own

I lived in my apartment for about a year before I even noticed that there was a store across the street from where I lived. I never opened my shade to look outside, and when I left, I went in the opposite direction of the store. The shopping mall and the grocery store I always went to were at the other end of the street, which is why I never bothered to look in the other direction. I was in my own little world and didn't want anyone or anything to overstep the boundaries I had finally learned to set. The kids and I were happy we had each other, but they missed their dad—and I missed him even though he was a batterer. I didn't know at the time that there were support systems available to assist me in dealing with my abusive situation.

My daughter couldn't understand why we couldn't be with her dad. It didn't matter if he was abusive to us or not, she really loved her dad and wanted me to forgive all of his faults. But that's a child for you; they just seem not to know any better. They want their parents to be with them no matter what. This is why some of us are parents and some are children waiting to grow up ourselves.

Children in unstable homes don't see the harm in a few ass-whippings here and there. They start to think this behavior is normal, because it isn't out of the ordinary for them. When you stay in an unstable home, the children learn to deal with the instability.

Children must have stability in their lives in order to grow and flourish. They are like plants. They have to be watered and nurtured, or they will wither up and die. Even after leaving Tony, I would let him come over and have sex with me. I didn't want the kids to see me with another man in the house and I needed to feel some kind of love (or what I thought it was), so I didn't date anyone else for fear they might try to abuse my children.

One evening my first cousin, Henry, came over. He used to live with Tony and I when we were still married, so I didn't think it unusual for him to come over for a visit. After he got into the house and sat down, I noticed that he had been drinking. He kept telling me how nice I looked since Tony and I had divorced.

Thinking nothing odd of this, I just said thank you and that the kids and I were getting along much better now. The kids were in bed at this time because it was around 9:30 p.m. The television was on and Henry grabbed the remote control and turned the volume up. I told him to turn it down because the children were asleep. He just started to laugh and came over and sat down on the couch by me.

I told him to move over because he was too close for me to feel comfortable. He was my first cousin, and family or no family; he didn't need to sit so close. Henry told me again how nice I looked. I asked him what his problem was, and why was he looking at me in such a seductive manner. He told me he would like to get it on with me. I told him he had to be kidding—he was my cousin. He said he had wanted to make love to me for some time. I asked him to leave, but by this time he was forcing himself on top of me.

I thought to myself, this couldn't be happening to me again. It was like a nightmare only it was real. I had begun to think that since I hadn't dealt with this sort of thing for such a long time, I thought it had become a part of my past.

As Henry started getting more and more aggressive during our struggle, I fought him with all my might. He said that if I didn't stop fighting him, he would go into the other room and bring my daughter into the front room to watch him rape me.

Of course, I didn't wish to have this happen, and I thought I could fight him off, but then I thought, what if he knocked me out and I lose consciousness? He might hurt my children as well. I decided to give in and get it over with. It wasn't as though I had not been in this type of situation before, and more than likely it wouldn't be the last time.

After my cousin had finished ejaculating, he climbed off me. I told him to get his clothes on and get the hell out of my house. I asked that he never visit me or speak to me again. I had been raped, but I didn't want to call the cops. This was my cousin and I didn't want to expose the children to a frightening scene when the police came. I was ashamed for my cousin and myself. It wasn't the first time I'd been raped, and I just wanted to forget it.

I took a long bath and hoped I could forget it had ever happened. The following morning, I phoned Tony and told him what had happened between Henry and I. He asked me if I wanted him to go after Henry. I said no, because it wouldn't help matters. I just wanted Tony to comfort me, and hold me and help me blot out the memories.

Several months went by and I started having morning sickness. I didn't think anything of the incident with my cousin, especially since Tony and I had continued to see one another. So when I told Tony I was going to the doctor to see why I was sick in the mornings he was glad, because he knew I must be pregnant again by him.

After the baby was born, he looked so much like me that Tony and I named him Cory. Tony and I never got back together after the baby was born, but he signed the birth certificate and paid child support for about a year for all three of the children.

He quit paying support for any of the kids, because he got fired from his job for doing drugs. He had also had a run-in with a coworker. He hit a coworker on the head with a steel pipe, because the co-worker had thrown a helmet at him and hit him in his face. Tony lost control and beat up his coworker, so he was asked to turn in his badge and leave.

As time went on, the more I looked at Cory the more he began to remind me of my cousin. I never talked to Tony about my hunch about Cory, but I talked to my stepmother about it. She told me to keep my thoughts to myself and never to mention it to anyone else again. What purpose would it serve anyone to know my feelings, she asked.

I let the nightmare die—or so I thought, until I found myself unable to work because I had let my mind become sick. I had dealt with so much with my ex-husband and his crap, in addition to the trauma of having Cory, I couldn't deal with my life anymore. He was a constant reminder of the traumatic experience. I couldn't concentrate or focus on my job, and I needed total focus to translate documents at work, so I applied for welfare. During that time the welfare system required applicants to fill out a mountain of papers. I quickly became tired of filling out papers and answering their questions.

I had always worked for a living and never before had accepted charity. I felt that if you were able to work, then you should work.

The welfare system told me that I couldn't have more than five hundred dollars in the bank at any given time, that my car could only be worth so much and that I couldn't have this or that. I couldn't live like that. I probably could have, but I chose not to. We all have choices to make in our lives and mine was to live independently. I wanted my children to have more out of life than welfare could afford to give them. I wanted them to have things I never had, like toys, clothes and anything I could afford to give to them.

They had already lost their father. Even though Tony didn't act like much of a father most of the time, he was around and had started helping with the bills. I decided to work on becoming a nude dancer, because my friend told me the money was good and the hours wouldn't get in the way of my time with my kids. This was a choice that I was making on my own, with no man holding his hand out or trying to claim he was my pimp daddy.

My friend told me about an agency on Lake Street that taught women how to become nude dancers. They provided the opportunity to get right to work onstage, to test your skills before a room full of people. If you got booed off the stage, then that was your problem not theirs, but if you were good enough to keep the audience's attention, you were off and running. That is exactly what happened to me. Dancing had always been a gift that came naturally for me. I loved to dance, so getting paid to do what I loved was a plus.

After filling out papers and an application, the agency sent me to a nude club in St. Paul where I auditioned to be a nude dancer. Dancing was never difficult for me because I loved doing it and was good at it. I just had never stripped before. We were behind glass, which made it much easier for me feel less self-conscious. I wasn't ashamed of my body. I was considered "stacked." My measurements at the time were 36-20-36. This was one profession I never dreamt I'd get paid to do, yet there I was: a nude dancer.

As time went on, I began to get into the groove of being a stripper. I started smoking a lot of marijuana, which helped me relax. I learned to block things out from my mind and I started enjoying my work. I learned to block out the fact that men might see me as a spectacle and how people in the audience glared at me.

I not only enjoyed dancing, but many people told I that I was a great dancer. Because I wasn't accustomed to being told I was good at many things, the attention made me feel proud of myself.

When I danced the room would fill up and I'd look over the heads and never really directly at them. The men seemed like animals, looking at me like they were eating me alive. As a dancer, I learned to swallow my pride and ignore the shame that came with this kind of job.

Why did I dance? I did it because my kids were safe. I adored them more than life itself. I had plenty of money to pay for the best babysitter. I never trusted many people, so I was fortunate enough to have my children's great-grandmother's housekeeper, Hazel, watch them. My kids were fed and taken care of, so who cares what people may think, I felt. People with that kind of attitude I could handle anytime. Every time I worked I told myself this same statement over and over again, yet deep down inside I was becoming sicker and sicker by the moment. I still wouldn't look back, I just kept on going.

I never drank when I worked at the strip joints, because I hated the smell of alcohol. Dating men was never part of my program either, at least not yet. I just went to work and collected my paycheck for doing the best job I could possibly do.

Lots of girls drank with the guys and dated them as well. They were being paid to have sex with men. I thought to myself, "I'm too good to let those men use me like some girls did." I never thought of bringing a guy home with me, because I didn't want men to be around my children. I didn't trust any of them, especially around my little girl.

I decided I wanted to start traveling. Some of the girls had told me that I could make a lot more money traveling, so I called an agent and he booked me to go to Canada within a week. I spoke with Hazel and she agreed to move in with us as a live-in nanny for my children. We agreed that we both would be more comfortable with this arrangement than letting some stranger watch my children.

This was the first time I had ever trusted anyone to watch my children other than my children's grandmother. I knew I could trust Hazel with my life—and my children's' lives. No one protects your children as well as you do, but I knew Hazel would do her darndest. I paid her a good wage and supplied all of the groceries.

Eventually, I began to call Hazel "Aunt Hazel." Hazel was always there for me. When I wasn't out of town, I spent most of my time with her and her family. Aunt Hazel never thought that a man should control a woman. I saw women with their pimps. These women not only let men control their lives, but their money as well. To some girls it seemed cool and made them want to try the glamorous life. Aunt Hazel's advised me against having a pimp. She was a very kind and loving person who had never needed to be controlled.

Hazel took excellent care of my children. One difference we had was around her belief in chastising and disciplining children. I believed no one had a right to spank my children, especially when I didn't do so myself. She believed that children should be seen and not heard around adults. When she was growing up as a child, she had been whipped with cords and belts. This made her harder on my kids, I believe, than the average person who didn't grow up with violence in the home.

I told her she didn't have my permission to hit my kids with anything except an open hand and only in moderation. If a child must be disciplined, I told her, it should be a tapping and not an actual spanking. I believe that if you can teach children to listen to what they are being asked to do, they will do it. As adults we must think how we would feel having someone tell us what to do, rather than being asked.

You should learn to use more "I statements" I told Aunt Hazel, and then my children would be more than open to listen to what is being said to them. Auntie and I struggled with this request, but she found over time that my children listened to whatever they were asked to do, because they had been taught to respect an adult's wishes.

All kids can get out of control sometimes, yet they can be controlled with a gentle hand rather than a heavy one. I taught my children to honor the parents who helped bring them into this world, and to understand that without their help they wouldn't be here.

I decided to leave town for two weeks and went to Canada to dance again. It was a large dance hall and bar. The Canadians were very nice to me, and I made excellent wages dancing, as well as tips from the customers. I still had not started dating customers.

I called my children every day and we would talk for an hour. They were in school during the day, and during the evenings Aunt Hazel was with them. She helped them with their homework. My kids were too young to figure out where I was going and what I was doing when I left town. If they asked me any questions, I would tell them that mommy had to work a lot to make enough money to pay bills. I informed them that it was hard for a woman to pay all the bills alone, especially since their father had chosen not to continue working and pay child support.

While I was in Canada, I had danced frequently at a bar called The Flame, located just outside of Canada on the Minnesota-Canadian border. They asked me if I would like to come and dance there for them, because the owner had seen me dance in Canada and liked my style. The owner said he would send a car over to get me whenever I was ready to come.

I loved dancing, even though I had to strip down to a g-string. I stood 5 feet 3 inches tall and weighed 110 pounds. People would tell me that I was pretty, but I never felt pretty. I always felt ashamed, because I knew deep down in my heart that I was not living totally right in the eyes of God. I believed all my life that I wanted to live a good clean life, so one day I would be able to go to heaven to be with my real mother. Swallowing my pride ate away at my insides, yet I continued on for my children. I could have survived on the kind of money I had made at the factory, but I would never been able to give them the kind of lifestyle they had because I danced. There were many times that I told myself that one day I would do something else, then I started making more money and put those thoughts on the back burner. Sometimes I questioned myself, wondering if I would ever change the way I was currently living.

Nothing mattered to me but my children having an abundant life. I felt that sometimes I was away from them too much, but I felt I must go on for their benefit. They needed to eat and be clothed. All of that cost money—and plenty of it—when you have three children. There were times when I told myself I was just acting and the movie would be over soon. That's how I was able to keep going a lot of days. I blocked everything out of my mind and didn't think about what I was really doing. I just kept saying to myself that things would eventually get better one day.

People may have judged me for my work, but they didn't know the real me. They judged me because of the type of work I did, and yet they forgot I was still a human as well. Dancing didn't make me a criminal, just someone working like everyone else and trying to make a living. I ask that I be judged for the person that I am, for the good that I have done—nothing more or less.

Dancing can be a beautiful profession, but it's all in the way you carry yourself. I have always tried to carry myself in a lady-like manner—in public and in private. And just because I was a dancer didn't mean that I went out to bars to pick up guys.

When I went out to have fun at nightclubs with my girlfriends, dancing was just for the fun of it because I loved to dance. After the dancing was over, so was the party for me. I'd go home alone. Drinking was never my cup of tea, either. I always need to be in control because I believe my mind is my only reality. I need to feel in control of most situations. This was my only defense: once I lost control, the fear would never end.

During my dancing career, many women came and watched me dance. They told me they loved to watch me dance and that I danced with grace, instead of the vulgarity that many other dancers showed in their style of dancing. I was seen as being more than an ordinary stripper; I was considered a performer.

After I was finished dancing the show was over for me. Because of the role-playing for this type of life, I was never myself. There are a lot of women who desire to be with other women. I was asked occasionally, but I never was moved to go in that direction. My preference was the male gender.

We all have things that we consider gray areas in our lives, and I am not one to put anyone down, because we all have to wear our own shames. We just know what shames we are willing to bear and which ones we are not. As for me, I am not here to judge anyone because I ask not to be judged.

I was really a shy individual, yet in real life I was "Lady Day." That's what my show name was anyway. Sometimes I went by the name of Candy, because many people told I was just too sweet to do what I was doing. Often I wondered what they meant. What was wrong with what I was doing? I was taking care of my children. They had a better life than they had ever known before.

After being gone for a few weeks, when it was time for me to head back home again, I looked forward to seeing my children. Sometimes I might sit out for a spell longer, but most times it was two weeks on and two weeks off. When I was home, my children and I went everywhere: the malls, parks, beaches....

I always tried to buy my children educational toys when we went shopping. Books were one of their favorites. I believed a strong mind was the most important thing to give a child. Without knowledge you don't seem to have much value in our society. I asked my kids to always do the best that they could possibly do. I wanted them to learn as much as possible.

Today, there are so many things out there for kids to take advantage of—things we didn't have the opportunity to experience as children, like "Hooked on Phonics," computer software and other learning tools that were inexpensive enough to buy. When you have a thirst for knowledge, there's no limit to what you can accomplish.

I believed that I was getting too old and had too many children to see getting an education as a way to get ahead. And, I never liked math, and for some reason no matter what course I wanted to take, math was always a part of the curriculum. I guess I had a math phobia.

7

New Adventures

I caught up with my friend, Jenny, who told me about a job opening at a massage parlor in Coon Rapids, a nearby suburb. I asked her what I had to do to get a job. Jenny showed me how to give a massage. After learning how to give one, I felt like a fool for needing to be taught because it seemed so simple.

At the parlor, sometimes men wanted to have sex with me, but it was my choice to have sex or not. After taking the job, I found that some men not only wanted to have sex, but some of them wanted to dress up like women themselves, among other things. Some of the things they'd ask me to do seemed so crazy, but the money was too good to pass up. If this was work, I thought, I should have been doing this a long time ago. There were men who would come into the sauna just to spend time with a girl, so they wouldn't be alone.

One time I came into the room where a customer was waiting. He had tied himself to the bed and had a gold ring around his little penis. It took all I had in me not to laugh at his fetish, instead, I said to him, "What do we have here my dear?" He was so thrilled that I had noticed his small cock.

I thought to myself about the work I was doing: "Wow, the things a person does for money." If I didn't care to be bothered or got the wrong feeling from a man, I would give a customer a massage and send him on his way. Some of the men were not what they appeared to be.

Most customers came in with one thing in mind: to get serviced so he could get out of the parlor as fast as he came in. If a man is willing to buy what he wants, he should be able to do so. When you are working, you aren't thinking about a man's wife or girlfriend. This isn't part of the job. I had learned to just be about taking care of my business at hand and not let my emotions come into play. The work I had chosen to do was about getting paid for a service—not about bringing feelings into the program at all.

No one had forced these men to come into the sauna; they came in by their own choice. Anyway, I thought, if I didn't take care of them another woman would. It was safer for the men to come in and see me than to take their chances on Lake Street with the street prostitutes.

Each of us has choices to make in life, when a customer came to me he had already made his choice to be there. They weren't hurting anyone, nor was I as a masseuse. Ladies, if the thought of sex with your spouse makes you sick to your stomach, you don't have to let them touch you, just send them on their merry little way and they will soon find us. Wouldn't you rather he get his rocks off with a working woman at a sauna and leave, not caring what happens to that women after he leaves her? Or would you prefer he find a mistress to fall in love with? When he leaves the sauna, at least you know that will normally be the end of the relationship.

The men we saw knew we were only in it for the money. There is no real satisfaction for the man, just momentary gratification. Life goes on to the next working day. The man will still come home to you, his wife or girlfriend. We used protection such as condoms, preventing passing on or getting a sexually transmitted disease. Going to a sauna is safer than having women who are working on the streets. The streets are where the real problems begin. These girls will rob and steal sometimes, as well as go without sexual protection.

A man might get angry and hurt a woman on the streets. What does the average person care about what tramp is walking the streets? It's not your child, right? Wrong thinking. How do you know it isn't? You don't. So many of those girls are hooked on drugs or with an abusive partner.

And even though she may work in a sauna or on the streets, doesn't mean that the rest of her life isn't normal—kids, rent, boyfriends…. What does the world consider a normal life, anyway? I know women today who are married and won't give their husbands a blowjob unless he buys her something special or gives her some money. Is this not a form of prostitution? So many women of the world are quick to judge a prostitute or a working woman, and yet they are providing a service to their boyfriends or husbands at a cost as well. So which one is right? The working woman or the wife/girlfriend? And, how many women are dating a married man and thinking nothing of it? So many women are quick to judge the work we do and are slow to live up to their own wrongs.

None of our paths are predetermined, especially not when you end up representing yourselves in the manner as a call girl. So, would you consider me a tramp or just a mother willing to do whatever it takes to care for her children?

Women tend to judge the ladies who work in saunas the harshest. But ladies the women don't go out and ask your husbands to come and seek them out. In fact, you may be pushing them to utilize those sorts or places. Why do men come to a sauna? Sometimes they want sexual pleasures that you aren't willing to give them. Some like to experiment with different sexual pleasures—pleasures that you aren't willing to explore. Men feel these experiences can take them to a different level of gratification.

You might be saying to yourself right now, "How in the hell does she know what she's talking about?" Because at one time I was a wife who told her husband that if he wanted to have oral sex, he had to go someplace else and get that urge taken care of. At that time in my life when I was married to Tony, I didn't believe that oral sex was a normal thing to do. Needless to say, he took me up on what I told him to do. Back then when I went to work, he had sex with the airline stewardess upstairs and when he couldn't get with her, he said he screwed the hooker down the hall. How do I know these things? Tony took pleasure in telling me this when I came home from work. All I could do at the time was cry, because I was the one who had told him to get it that way. I could have left him at the time, but I thought that I was still too much in love with him. So, ladies, think about what I am telling you before you run your husbands off to a sauna.

At times, I felt because of the incest in my past, I was pushed into a profession I didn't want to be in. I had never felt worthy of much. My self-worth was sucked right out of me during those days when I began to think it was all right for my stepbrothers to molest me.

A lot of money has been wasted trying to control the sex industry. No matter how much money is spent trying to stop prostitution, it will always be with us.

I learned no one has a right to force me to have sex. There are children being forced to have sex every day because a mother (or father) is too blinded by the slick ways of a husband or boyfriend (or wife/girlfriend) to even notice the warning signs. Sometimes the signs are right before her eyes, but she refuses to see the signs for fear of not having a roof over their heads.

But what is a roof without structure? Will it stop the raindrops from falling within? I don't think so. Nor will ignoring the pain change the sorrow within your child's heart. This is why I watched my children like a hawk for fear of the unknown possibilities.

During my working profession, I never missed taking my children to the clinic for their immunizations or a parent teacher's conference. If they were in sports, I went to their games whenever I could. I didn't really care for watching sports much, but I cared enough to be there to support them.

Children need at least one (preferably both) parent's support to help them feel worthy and loved. I knew what it felt like to have no one love me most of my life. I was determined to not have my children walking around with the same feelings locked up inside of them that I did.

8

The Fast Life

Fast money, fast cars, fast living. That's what you do when you make quick money. And the money leaves as fast as you make it. Money can take you to so many different levels in life.

There I was, this shy little kitten who had just begun to get her feet wet. I thought I was so darned smart and knowledgeable. I believed I would never let some smooth-talking asshole choose me. What I didn't know at the time was that no matter how smart we believe we are, there is always someone out there who believes they are smarter.

During the beginning stages of my life in the fast lane, I found out quickly what a so-called pimp was. I was working in a sauna, without a pimp's help and along comes some guy telling me that I need him to manage my money and that he will protect me. How can he protect me when he is at home or on the streets having a good time with someone else? He said that he'd be waiting for me to bring the money home to "daddy" (what the pimps called themselves).

I didn't really know what a pimp was until I came to Minnesota. I had read the book *Iceberg Slim* when I was a teenager. My stepmother had a copy on the story of his life and I just happened to pick it up one day and started reading it. How fascinating, I thought: one guy with all those different women. How could you share a man you loved without feeling cheated, I thought to myself. I would have kicked his ass as well as hers if he ever thought he could fuck some bitch in my presence. He must be crazy, I thought.

My boss at the sauna, Robert, had evidently struck an interest in me. I didn't pay much attention to him, because he already had a woman. I wasn't the type of woman who believed in sharing her man with anyone else. I was a jealous woman who was known by many as a fighter, as well. I would've kicked a woman's ass at the drop of a hat, if she came too close to my man.

I wasn't taking much shit off anyone at this point in my life. Being in the fast life had begun to harden me inside. And, as a single woman with kids, I was always suspicious of everyone I met. I was careful with my personal relations, because if anything were to happen to me, who would take care of my children? I learned to always be on my guard and leery of everyone.

On this particular evening, my boss asked me to go out with him and just because I wasn't doing anything, I said, "Why not?" He came by Aunt Hazel's and picked me up in his Lincoln Continental. Robert had a beautiful car. It was so big I thought someone could probably actually live in it. He must drive around banging all the bitches he could handle, I thought to myself.

Boy, was I ever wrong about this man. I thought he couldn't be a very nice person because of the things I had read or had learned about other men considered pimps. Robert didn't fit the profile at all. I had misjudged him. He was handsome and very polite. He opened the door for me and made sure I was seated comfortably in the car, and then he asked me what we should do. This surprised me, because I didn't think I had a choice in the matter. I told him it was entirely up to him, because he was the one who was supposed to be taking me out.

He took me to the top of an exquisite hotel in downtown Minneapolis where he wined and dined me. We ate lobster and steak and he had a drink. We enjoyed each other's company very much. Later on that evening he took me by his place. I figured this was his way of assuring me that he didn't have a woman living with him. You can believe that I gave the house the once-over when we were inside to settle my own mind.

He had a very nice home with black and gold furniture in his living room and a huge marble table in the dining room. Everything looked so expensive. He showed me his bedroom. There were mirrors everywhere. I thought I had never seen a home lovelier than his.

The evening was coming to an end and neither of us wanted to end the moment. I told him that I would be more than glad to see him again. He drove me back to Aunt Hazel's house. The following morning I got up with the kids to get them ready for school. Just as I was going back to bed, the phone rang. It was Robert! He asked me if I was awake yet and if he could visit me. I told him that I didn't see people at my home because of my children. He told me he'd pick me up, so we could go for a ride. During our drive, we went to a beautiful apartment complex, which had an indoor pool, a sauna and an exercise room.

I asked Robert who lived there. He told me it was a gift for me. I laughed, but he was very serious. He had really paid for it for me for the first six months in advance, and he had filled it with beautiful furniture. It was all for me. I couldn't believe someone would ever care enough about me to do something like this. He said he knew the owner of the building and together they had fixed it up—lock, stock and barrel.

After giving me the keys, he told me he would see me later and for me to get acquainted with my new "home-away-from-home." After he left, I turned on the television, laid back on my beautiful leather couch and fell fast asleep. I was awakened when Robert kissed me on my forehead. I greeted him with a big hug to show my appreciation. No one had ever treated me this way. I asked Robert what this kind of treatment meant and what his expectations of me were in return.

Robert told me that he just wanted a little bit of my time. He said he didn't expect me to sleep with him because he had paid for an apartment. He wanted to spend as much time with me as he could. This was one thing we both agreed on, because I wanted to spend more time with him, too.

Most women would have enjoyed getting to know him because he was gorgeous—very tall and slender. He was about 6 feet tall and had been a model for several stores in New York City.

As time went on, I became very fond of this interesting man. He was a hard worker and enjoyed having me by his side. Robert wasn't working at the sauna, he was partnering with someone else and working as a co-owner of another sauna. Robert decided to break up with his former lady. I wasn't the cause of their breakup with one another. Their relationship had been on the outs for a long time before I came into the picture, according to the other girls I worked with. I was happy that I wasn't the cause, because I'd never been the type to steal another women's man.

Robert and I stayed together most of our spare time. He loved taking me out on the town and showing me off to all of his friends. He was proud to have me as his one and only woman. There were plenty of men who wanted to get to know me, yet I was devoted to my man with all of my heart. I never gave any of them the time of day.

I had found that some men just wanted a woman, so she'd break down and have sex with one of them. Then they'd brag about it to all of their friends. This seemed to make them feel like they had very large balls. Other times they would ride around in their fancy cars, bragging to their buddies over and over about how they fucked the shit out of some other brother's woman. They would ride around in their fancy cars, trying to pull more women than their friends. Life in the fast lane was kicking, with plenty of time to see who could out-do the other—more women, more cars, boats and clothes. There was no end to their madness. The pimps and whores all thought they had it going on in Minnesota at that time in the early 1980s.

I was making lots and lots of money, because Robert had me working at the sauna as well as managing it. He paid me a handsome salary for managing the sauna. He wined and dined me most evenings. We seemed to have a very strong and long-term relationship. I was waiting for the moment when Robert would ask me to pay him for his services, but it never happened. When a man is making love to you and he is in the game, there comes a time when it is time for you to pay up for services rendered, (meaning that kind of servicing, this is why they were considered pimps). I thought for a long time that this was the way it was eventually going to be. When you run into people living in the fast lane, you assume in time that the move will be made on you to start producing the dollars for their services.

When we were out on the town, the ladies would try to get Robert's attention by making eyes at him. He always put them in their place by letting them know I was his woman, and at present he was not looking for any new seekers.

One evening the lady he used to be with came up and said hello to him. He said, "Bitch, you know the name of the game, and you don't speak to me unless I acknowledge you first."

"Are you here to choose a man or not? Where are you coming from? Do you have any trap?" Robert asked her. He wanted to know if she had any money to hand over to him, not for services rendered, but for just the fact that she wanted to have a conversation with him. Time is money.

"No," she said.

"I didn't think so," he said, "You had better get the hell out of my face and run along." She stood there seemingly stunned at his reaction.

She finally left when Robert asked her if she wanted him to kick her stupid ass all over the place. I couldn't believe the way he was acting toward a woman who had been with him for a long time.

He was being disrespectful, but he also acted as though he was looking for another woman to be with the two of us. I wasn't sure if he was trying to impress the other assholes by standing his ground while we were in public or what to think. Status was a huge thing when you were out "representing" among the boys.

I was deluded into believing that being with Robert was one of the best things that had ever happened to me. I thought that he adored me. He may have, but from the moment he found out that I was pregnant, he didn't want to have anything to do with me. He said that I had let it happen on purpose and I must have planned the whole thing to trap him. I tried to explain to him that I really didn't plan on it happening, because I didn't want to have any children as an unmarried woman. Neither of us had been using any protection. I thought nothing of this because it seemed that I never got pregnant except once every three years. I didn't think I was in the cycle for pregnancy to happen.

I told him to get the hell out of my apartment. He refused and then hauled off and slapped me for the first time. He had never acted before like he would hit me. I drew back my fist and I punched him as hard as I could. He slapped me across my face again and I began to cry.

My state of emotions didn't move him in the least. Men can act like animals at times, when they act as if they have no emotions unless it benefits them. How can a man tell you that he loves you in one breath, and in the next you mean less than nothing because you've become pregnant? He thought I wanted his precious money because he owned a whorehouse.

He asked me to get rid of the child. I told him that I refused to have an abortion and that was my final answer, then I told him to get the hell out of my apartment and don't let the door hit him in the ass on the way out.

As I became bigger during my pregnancy, I had to quit working. I didn't see much of Robert after that; he made himself very scarce. I know he felt bad about the way he had treated me.

Some men think with their dicks, not their minds. My mom told me that a man's cock had no conscious and it is his glory. He runs around holding it in his hand most of the time. The life that I was living at the time didn't let me put much trust in a relationship.

There were times when Auntie wouldn't leave my side, even if it meant placing her own life in danger. She wanted to confront anyone who hurt me—at any level. During my pregnancy, someone had kicked in the door of my apartment. Auntie stayed at the apartment with me, because the door was being held by only one set of hinges. I didn't know who had kicked in the door or if they would come back and try and finish the job. The lazy landlord didn't fix it for quite some time.

Aunt Hazel went with me to the hospital and stayed with me throughout labor and delivery. Auntie was my source of strength and support, and she was always there for me no matter what situation I was in.

During the delivery, the doctors asked me if they could bring in about eight college students to watch my child's birth. The delivery went well and my son was born in the wee hours of the morning, screaming loudly (and he has been that way ever since).

I let Aunt Hazel help me pick a name for him. I gave him his first name, Rashad, and she gave him his middle name, Jabez, which came from the Bible.

9

Mr. Smooth

Life goes on and I had to move on with my life after Robert. He was gone and I had to face the reality of my situation. I was a woman in charge of my own life and the mistakes that came with it. I had no choice but to accept my situation: a brand new baby, no husband and no job. I felt alone once again, with no one to turn to but my limited resources and myself.

My ex-husband had been remarried several years, and I had given him and his wife temporary custody of our three children. Having met his new wife shortly after they were married, I realized that she was a very responsible and likable person. I was surprised Tony had found someone as nice as her. She was about five years older than him and had a good-paying job. Tony was doing well too at his job, so the kids lived well with them during the school year.

I kept the kids on the holidays and weekends. Having my weekdays free gave me time to be out in the limelight again. I went back to working at a sauna, dodging all the pimps, wimps and simps out there looking for some fresh bait to trap. The pimps called me an "outlaw bitch" because I chose not to have a man. It was by choice that I didn't want a man at this particular time in my life. I asked myself, "Why would I want a man?" For what, so he could count my dollars and spend my hard-earned money? This didn't make any sense to me. The pimps chased women down like animals in heat, but all a pimp wants is a girl's money. If a girl quit working while being with a pimp, he would leave her quicker than she could say "Jack Flash." Ladies, if you work in the business, be smart and save all the money you can. You never know when the pimps or the system will destroy your lives.

When I was working in the so-called fast life, there was rampant abuse of the girls by pimps. They would kidnap them, take their money and make some of them work day and night. The women were so frightened that they would do whatever the pimp told them to do. Sometimes a pimp would tell a woman not to come home unless she had $200 or $300 dollars of trap money a night.

A girlfriend had been a dancer for her man for about fourteen years. She was making $1,500 to $2,000 a week. He wouldn't let her buy herself a 50-cent White Castle hamburger. He had to use all of her money for smoking crack cocaine with his buddies, and wouldn't even let her hit the pipe. I asked her why she put up with that kind of bullshit, because I wouldn't. She told me that she loved him so much and she didn't want to live without him. That type of love sickens me to my stomach. Killing ourselves doesn't change a man like that's way of thinking; he just goes on to his next victim. End the cycle of abuse before accepting the second slap, because you can rest assured it is coming.

Seeing things like this happening around me made me think hard before I got involved with another man. Whenever I was out with the girls, I would be on my guard. I learned to never look a pimp in his eyes, because if you looked him in his eyes it meant that you were ready to choose him.

One pimp went around bragging about how he was sticking broken bottles up his lady's pussy. This was real funny to him and he was proud of himself. Evidently, to him this showed he was a real man with large balls. How stupid could he be? If he sticks a broken bottle up his woman's pussy, how can she work?

Whenever a pimp approached me and told me that I should choose, I would say, "Choose what? A simple-minded nobody like yourself?" I didn't need anyone telling me how to spend my money, how to make it or where to stash it. I asked him why doesn't he go down on Lake Street and bend his ass over and get busy, because he can take it in his ass just as quick if not quicker than I could in the front. I didn't worry about being beaten up by a pimp because I knew that sometimes I had to talk tough, or the wolves would've eaten me up. If I was going to dance with them, then I knew I had better learn how to play the game better than them. They called me a crazy bitch and said that I had big balls. "Crazy" because I had a brain of my own and wasn't swayed by their charms, and that I had turned myself out in this nasty business. I got into the fast life without a pimp, and I never had a pimp collecting my money.

Ladies, you don't need any man telling you how to spend your money. When your body starts falling apart, you can bet he won't be anywhere to be found. He'll be between some other woman's legs trying to get his rocks off, because he doesn't give a damn where you are after you leave home to work. Keep it real and try to be true to yourself before being true to anyone else.

While visiting the local Establishment Nightclub, I saw a man who caught my eye. I thought he was darling, and I loved the way he carried himself. He always dressed so nicely. He was a clean-cut, all-around tailored kind of guy. I called him Mr. Smooth. He was so smooth that he could make ice cream melt at least that's what I thought at the time.

I was watching Mr. Smooth, and he was watching me, too. This little chase went on for several months. Every weekend I would visit the club and he would be there. He was always looking good, and always alone with no woman in sight. The ladies loved trying to cozy up to this gentleman, but he showed no interest in them whatsoever. This made me all the more interested in him. I thought to myself, he couldn't be a pimp. He seemed too nice to be that type of person, because most of them weren't anything nice. Who's to say what type of person a pimp really is, I wondered. My curiosity was getting the best of me and I wanted to get to know this man.

I needed to be careful not to get caught up in his game. At the time, I was managing and working in a sauna in Fridley. I was also still working at a large insurance company in downtown Minneapolis in the central transcription department, translating documents. That didn't leave me much time to play around. I felt I needed the money for my children and I.

While working for the insurance company, I filed a discrimination lawsuit because when I applied for a permanent job, they didn't want to hire me. This didn't make much sense, given my history at the company. I had started working for the company on a temporary basis through a secretarial pool. My qualifications more than fulfilled the job requirements. They hired me for a two-week project that ended up lasting more than three months. They said they kept me on because I was doing such a great job.

The department head had asked me to apply for the full-time position. She told me that I knew the job inside and out and that I was a great candidate for the job. On the day of my interview, I waited for about an hour and a half in the human resources office. Suddenly a nice-looking, blonde-haired lady arrived in the office. As she approached the desk, she was greeted warmly. She came back and sat down right next to me. I left my seat and went up to the desk to ask the receptionist if the woman who had just arrived was being seen first. She said yes. She told me that the woman had gotten lost and that her interview was scheduled ahead of mine.

I sat back down to wait my turn. The blonde lady asked me if human resources were going to see her before me. I said yes. She took out a piece of paper and wrote her name and phone number down on it. She told me if I decided ever to do something about the matter to give her a call. She chose not to be interviewed and left. This lady didn't even know me. She was white and I am black. She told me she wouldn't work for a company that discriminated. I felt a lot of respect for her, even though I didn't know anything else about her.

I wish I could thank her for what was in store for me. I had walked away from so many other companies because of racial slurs or just blatant disrespect. I could always tell when someone is acting like they have a problem with me because of my color. After a while I got accustomed to people acting that way. If it had not been for what the blonde-haired woman said to me in that office that day, I would have just called it another lost day.

I've found that being black sometimes destroys your chance at even being considered for a job. After encountering discrimination, as African Americans we come to expect to be treated in this manner. I often wonder why I can't be judged on my qualifications like the next person who is from a different race? Life can be so evil and hard to handle at times. There should be more people like the blonde lady in this world. It would be a much better place to live in.

After making me wait a while longer, the company eventually let me try out for the job. Later they told me someone else had been hired for the position.

I went to the agency that the blonde lady had told me about to contest my not being hired. I told an advocate about my situation from beginning to end. The representative confirmed my suspicions: they were being racist and it could be proven. I gave the representative the lady's name of which I had met briefly while waiting for my interview. I told her that she was a white lady—someone who didn't even know me. I told the advocate how she hadn't liked the way I had been treated and didn't want to be interviewed by a racist organization.

I explained to her that I had worked for this company by request for three months and it wasn't until I tried to apply for a permanent full-time position that the door to opportunity had been shut. I told her it was my understanding that when a company hired someone to do a job and if they didn't do the job properly, they would have reason to fire the person, especially if their qualifications didn't meet the company's expectations. Anyone with common sense knows not to keep a temporary employee on the job for three months or more if that person's performance isn't meeting the job requirements.

The lady from the agency checked into the background of the company and her findings backed up our suspicions. Primarily white people, with a few token minorities, staffed the company. They had only one black department head: my old boss. That's why I had originally thought there wouldn't be a problem in my being hired. Because my boss was black, I assumed that they would hire another black person without hesitation.

The lady at the agency eventually informed me that I had been awarded the job, if I wanted it. The choice was mine to make. I could take the job or I could choose to have them pay me for the three months I had waited to be hired. I chose to take the job to prove my point.

After completing my probationary period of six months, I wrote a letter of resignation. The manager of personnel called me down to his office and asked me what correspondence school I had graduated from. I said none. I told him that a previous employer had taught to me to write through an on-the-job training program.

He asked me if he could have me trained to become a correspondent. I told him that I had taken the job to prove a point: I was overqualified for the position and I had passed my probation with flying colors. I told him if I had accepted the job under better circumstances, I would be more than glad to accept his offer, but due to the circumstances I had no choice but to resign. Why benefit a company that didn't want to hire me in the first place?

For me, it's my principles that motivate me to what I do. I believe society should judge people on their merits—nothing more, nothing less. Color doesn't automatically make a person good or bad. Pride also has played a large role in my life. When you grow up with so much shame and disappointment in your life, many times all you have to stand on is your pride.

I have always tried to be very real and up front sort of person. If someone asks me a question or for my opinion, I strive to be truthful and to the point. And, when I am working at a job, I devote all of my time and attention to that job. I want to do the best job that I can do for myself, if no one else.

Choosing Mr. Smooth was so cool (for him anyway). He played me like a toy. I thought I was so smart I'd never get caught by anyone's net. Mr. Smooth had been so smooth—all the way up to his capture of me. After I had given him the time of day, he played his role of Mr. Nice Guy. Mr. Smooth started out our lit-tle romance by wining and dining me at the different hot spots in Minneapolis. He wanted everyone to know that he had captured me. Many men had tried to sway me into their nest, but their smooth-talking lines hadn't moved me.

I thought Mr. Smooth was different: He had a Journeyman's Painters License. There was no way for me to know that he was a pimp as well. He had never had a lady on his arm during the entire two years I had watched him from across the bar. He drove me to his apartment one evening to show me where he lived. He cooked dinner for us and massaged my feet afterward. My, was he handsome, I thought. I loved the way this man treated me from the very beginning, and I thought I could easily fall in love with him.

I wanted to take things one day at a time and move slowly in this relationship, because I didn't want to get burned again. I was over Robert and wanted a new man in my life. My son, Rashad, was about three years old by now.

Mr. Smooth had never let on that he knew what type of work I was doing. After being in the relationship for only three months, the party was already almost over for us. Mr. Smooth took me shopping and bought me about twenty different sexy outfits. He told me to try them on and model them for him. He told me I looked so good that he just wanted to "fuck the shit out of my little fine ass."

I figured it had been long enough since we first started seeing one another. He had never acted like a pimp up to this point, so why should assumed he was a pimp. We had been seeing one another for three months. I thought, why not let him make love to me?

I knew he had to have a huge cock, because whenever we slow danced, I would always feel the bulge. We went into the bedroom and the lights were very dim as he started to undress me. As he took off his underwear, a chill went up my spine. His cock was so huge. I thought to myself that if he put it in me that it would tear me open. He saw the expression on my face and told me to not be afraid. He would put it in slowly. He asked to be excused for a moment. I thought he was going to get some lubrication. Boy, was I ever wrong. When he got back into the bed, he told me to close my eyes, he had a big surprise for me.

When I closed my eyes a cold chill ran over my body. I had never trusted any-one, so I quickly opened my eyes as I felt a sharp, hard object between my legs. I opened my eyes in a panic to find he had inserted a .45 magnum gun into my vagina. My first thought was, "What kind of freak have I gotten involved with this time?" I started to cry, but to pimps like Mr. Smooth, tears meant nothing and he had no remorse for what he had done to me.

I had been strung along by a real smooth pimp this time, one who really knew how to play the game better than anyone I had ever came in contact with before. Sometimes we get what we deserve, but what had I ever done to deserve this?

That night Mr. Smooth made love to me as no one had ever had love made to me before. As usual, I thought to myself, here I go again: another sexual act without feelings. I had played this game so long that I never expected to have an orgasm. I didn't have sex to feel good; it was to satisfy my man.

He said I had chosen him because he had inserted the gun into my vagina. In the fast life, you know you're chosen when you find yourself in this kind of situation. This is the game of pimps and whores, and that is how they treat you. I had never considered myself a whore, because I was considered a high-class call girl. I asked him why he thought I would want to choose him as my man, because who needed a man telling me how to manage my money. I told him he had nothing to do with making the money, nor could he protect me if anything happened to me as I was working. He responded with more of his fiction, saying he would protect me and that he was keeping his eye on me. In this game that I had gotten myself mixed up in, the gun incident just got blown off after a couple of days.

The money I made was to support my son, Rashad, who was being cared for by Aunt Hazel. I would constantly pick him up or go to Aunt Hazel's to spend time with him. My other kids were still living with their father and stepmother. Rashad was my only major concern. I wasn't going to let anyone stand in the way of my giving him everything he could ever want.

I had no desire to be controlled by a pimp or live the type of life I knew many of them lived. For the first time in my life, I was afraid for my life and I didn't know what to do about the situation I had gotten myself in. The only thing I knew to do was to keep going to work.

I never told Aunt Hazel what had happened between Mr. Smooth and I. Aunt Hazel would have gone after him, I believe, with her gun in hand. She probably would have shot him, because she didn't take any shit off anyone. She wouldn't have let him get away with it.

As time went on, Mr. Smooth never checked my trap to see how much money I had made each day. He told me to give him whatever I wanted him to have. I thought that was a strange request. Why would I want him to have anything he didn't work for and why should he help me spend it?

Besides the fact that he was a pimp, I had another rude awakening. One morning Mr. Smooth entered the bedroom and told me he had something to tell me. I asked him what was so important that he had to wake me up so early. I had worked late the night before and was awfully tired because I had seen ten customers. Many of the massages I gave were referred to as hard massage. (We called them hard massages, not deep massages because they weren't therapeutic massages.)

I really didn't feel like taking any crap from him so early in the morning. He told me I would be meeting my "wife-in-law" later that evening. I asked him what a wife-in-law was. He said she was his other woman, who was also black and would be over later that night. I hated the idea because I wasn't accustomed to sharing my man with anyone. I didn't say no because I was afraid of Smooth by now, and I didn't know what his reaction would be.

When I met his wife-in-law, Helen, that night, she said she had been out "making daddy some money" before she arrived. She wanted to keep daddy happy, she said. I thought to myself that she was really not all there, because Mr. Smooth was not her daddy. I knew that "daddy" wasn't happy with the amount of money she had shared with him, because they started to argue. I really didn't care to find out what that was all about, so I decided to keep quiet.

Evidently another man had told Mr. Smooth about Helen flirting with some guy, and that maybe she had given the other man some of her money. Mr. Smooth hit her in her jaw with a closed fist. I couldn't believe he had the nerve to do something like that to a woman. She didn't take his abuse lying down. She leaped back at him like a dog in heat. He punched her in the stomach so hard, I thought he had killed her. Helen got up from the floor and told him how much she still loved him.

I asked myself, what kind of a damn nut was he dealing with? How could a man want a woman like this? She seemed up and down like the weather. Was she worth the ride? I didn't think so. When it comes to the game, men feel money has no name or shame. Most men will tolerate a lot of bullshit when it puts a few dollars more in their pocket.

Helen turned out to be a real winner. There were times when Mr. Smooth and I would enter the Establishment Night Club only to find her in some other guy's face. She was just grinning and skinning and shaking her big, black self all over the floor. This behavior was Helen's demise.

It's a known fact in the business that when you are with a man (pimp), you should never make eye contact with another pimp—let alone be up in his face. Helen knew this was a forbidden thing to do. She didn't seem to care. She seemed to like it when Smooth was kicking her ass around the clubs. In her mind, this proved that he really loved her, because it was the only time he took the time to pay attention to her.

One night after watching her act this way, Smooth went up and grabbed her by her throat. He carried her outside, where he kicked her ass all up and down the street. At the club, no one meddled in anyone else's business, and especially when a woman screamed. Most times it is just ignored. Nobody seemed to want to come to her rescue, not even the man she had been flirting with. When Helen came back into the bar, her face was bloody and red as a beet. I asked her to let me take her to the bathroom and get her washed up.

Helen and I never had anything against one another. We were just two women caught up in the same game. Both of us had fallen in love with the same asshole and the only difference between her and I was that I didn't ask for ass-whippings. I never liked sharing a man, but what damn difference did it make? Men said they didn't have another woman, and then down the line you find out they were liars. We both knew Mr. Smooth couldn't love us both. He just loved what we did for him.

After arriving home, Smooth told me he was done with that stupid bitch and it would just be he and I from now on. He had decided he'd had enough of Helen for a lifetime.

One night when Mr. Smooth and I arrived at the club, Helen saw us enter the room and came right over to say hello to Smooth. He told her, "Cunt, you should get the hell away from me before I kick the shit out of your stupid, worthless ass." Helen said, "I am going to kick your other woman's ass tonight." He told her to go ahead and try.

Helen told me she would catch me later. I said, "Bitch, you don't know me well enough to even want to go there." She didn't know that I was a fighter, and that if was by choice that I not act a fool. I was older and had stopped fighting over men some time ago.

One night I was outside the bar in the car waiting for Mr. Smooth to stop talking to his buddies, when suddenly Helen approached my window and tried to take a swing at me through the window. Mr. Smooth saw what she had tried, ran over, grabbed her by her neck and tried to choke her.

She started screaming bloody murder. Some bystander tried to help her and Mr. Smooth went crazy. He beat that man down to the ground like a madman gone crazy. After he finished beating the man down, he beat Helen, who had been waiting to see if the other guy could handle Smooth. He walked away and left both of them lying on the sidewalk, got into the car without saying a word and drove home. I kept my mouth shut, glad that I wasn't the one getting the ass whipping.

That night he made passionate love to me and told me that he loved me—I mean, really loved me. He said he would never hit me the way he hit her. This much I knew was true, not because I believed he loved me but because he knew I was too cool to ask for that kind of an ass whipping. If I never got out of line, why would he have to put me in check like that?

Smooth and I became very close and our love strong. We were just like a normal couple, I thought.

I arrived home from work one night not long after the incident with Helen very happy, and I wanted Smooth to know how much I loved him. He had made me so happy when he dumped that nutcase of a woman. I wanted to do something nice for him in return. I had made a lot of money that night and I wanted to give Smooth most of it, especially since I had already put away a lot of money for Rashad and myself. He couldn't believe it. He was at a loss for words. I was giving him an entire day's earnings. This particular day I wanted him to feel special.

Later that night, I walked into the bedroom only to find him and two other guys with some kind of white powder. I knew from what I had heard about drugs that this must be cocaine. I never even suspected that Smooth did the stuff. They had a razor blade, some one-fifty-one rum and a torch.

Mr. Smooth put some rum into a small glass jar. He then put the cocaine in and some baking soda. He said it was to help it "cook and rock up." I had no idea what he was referring to at the time, because I had never seen cocaine before. I didn't even drink, let alone do any cocaine or "crack."

They had a glass pipe with a net in the pipe. They put the "crack" on top of the net and torched it, inhaling the smoke deeply and holding their breath. They looked so funny with their eyes bulging out of their sockets that I laughed at them. Mr. Smooth told me to take a puff. I told him there was no way I was going to do any cocaine.

The only drug that I did at that time was a little pot every now and then—and that was only one or two hits on a joint. Smooth crumbled some crack into a joint. He called it a mackenball. He told me that I would like it.

Knowing that he might be upset if I didn't do as he asked me to do in front of his friends, I pulled on it as if I was smoking a regular joint. He told me to hold the smoke in; it worked better that way. I took a few more pulls and discovered that I liked the taste of it. It made me feel so good inside.

We were up half the night smoking crack. Smooth had taught me how to smoke crack in a matter of hours. I felt so freaky, sort of sexy, and wanted to make love to my man. My heart started racing and I became paranoid. After his friends left, he told me to get undressed and he started to go down on me. It felt so darned good. I wanted to scream with pleasure. I started to squirm like an animal in heat. I thought I could never enjoy someone doing this to me, but I loved it. I didn't seem to be myself; it was as though I was someone else. Feeling freaky was new for me because I had never really felt that way before.

I felt like a person with great strength and power. No one could harm me when I felt so damn good. We had an evening I wouldn't soon forget. The next morning Mr. Smooth went to get some more crack so that we could celebrate my rude awakening. He thought I was so "cute" when I smoked crack. I thought that we must be going crazy, but I wanted to do it again. I didn't act like a normal person when I was doing this stuff. It made me feel like some sort of freak. Sometimes my heart would beat so rapidly that I didn't know what to do. I'd get nervous and pray to come down off the high.

The party was on that whole week with Mr. Smooth and I. I thought the fun would never end, but let's get real, you can only do so much cocaine before your money starts to run low. It was time to make some more money.

My honeymoon with crack was over and reality was staring me in the face. When I came home from work that evening, Smooth had some crack waiting and wanted me to have a good time. I just wanted to rest.

He started inviting his friends over to get high with him, since I was too tired most times. They would come over and smoke up all the money I made selling my ass. I asked myself, how in the world could he do something like this to me, especially since I had been so good to him? How could he treat me like a butt wipe? I didn't appreciate this kind of disrespect. I wouldn't accept this treatment from any man of mine. I went to the neighborhood dealer, picked up some crack, bought all the things Mr. Smooth daddy had shown me, and smoked up a storm all by my little old lonesome.

I felt as though I didn't need him anymore—not as long as I had my pipe. Just give me a closet or a quiet room and the party was about to begin. Who needs friends when you have your shit, not me, ha!

10

The Break

One day I had Rashad with me at home. Usually, Rashad was at Aunt Hazel's when I was planning on smoking. I knew I wasn't going to be naughty that day, because I had my son with me and I was always responsible when he was around. I never let my children know that I ever did drugs. I didn't want them around the negative influence of drugs. Even if you are a softhearted person to begin with, drugs can make you hard.

Instinct was a source of survival for me in the fast life. Through it all, I never lost sight of my direction. I never lost my self-control. I liked getting high sometimes, but not to the point of not knowing what I would do next. There has always been a limit to my madness. I can only be led astray so long. I need control of my mind at all times. People who become crackheads let themselves be taken far beyond that point. They become weak from the drugs, and then the drugs work like the devil devouring their victim mentally and physically.

One night, Mr. Smooth was in St. Louis visiting his mother. At about five o'clock in the morning I heard what sounded like breaking glass coming from the living room. Rashad and I were in the bedroom. Rashad was still fast asleep. I went into the living room and caught Helen climbing through the window. Our apartment was on the first level, making it was easy for her to climb into the apartment after breaking the window. I asked Helen what did she thought she was doing. She said she had come to kick my ass. As she came toward me, I grabbed Rashad and put him in the apartment hallway so he wouldn't get hurt. He started to cry, so nutcase Helen said we should stop fighting so I could tend to him.

At this point, there was no way I was going to stop, so I lit into her. After I felt she had truly had enough, I ended the fight. I didn't end it for her sake. She had been asking for it for a long time, because she loved to start shit. This was one of the main reasons Mr. Smooth had left her in the first place.

I told her to go back into the apartment and get the record she had been whining about leaving at our place. I needed to go to the landlord's office to find out about getting the window replaced. Helen got her record and joined me on my way to the caretaker's apartment. That nut said that she was sorry for what she had done, and then asked me if I had a joint to smoke with her. I couldn't believe she had asked me to smoke right after we fought, but that was Helen for you. She always had to be starting something, even though she had been gone from our scene for a long time. I asked her if she thought Mr. Smooth's dick was gold-plated, and when she said yes I thought I would keel over and die.

I told Helen she was way out on a limb. She said so what, that's how she felt about him. This made me think they really were made for one another. She said she knew that he loved me and not her, but so what. I said Smooth doesn't love either of us; he loved what we did for him. I said he was probably down in St. Louis with his main squeeze, and we were probably just two more of his stooges.

I never fooled myself into thinking that a pimp was in love with me. That was just not the way the game was usually played. If he were so concerned about my well-being, he would have showed in his actions by treating me with respect rather than disrespecting me when he chose a new wife-in-law.

When Mr. Smooth daddy came back home from St. Louis, I had a big surprise for him. Rashad was at Aunt Hazel's. I told Mr. Smooth what Helen had done while he was away in St. Louis. Smooth couldn't believe she had the nerve to do something like that.

Later that evening, Helen phoned and told him she wanted to come by and talk with him. He told her she would have to wait for a few hours, since he had just gotten back into town and then she was welcome to come by later.

I knew how upset Smooth was about Helen's break-in and that when she arrived he was going to kick her ass. As soon as she walked into the door of the apartment, the fight was on. I told him to leave the girl alone. He told me to shut up. I told him that he was hurting her and that he needed to stop before he hurt her seriously.

Smooth told me to take my ass into the other room and sit down on the couch and be quiet. I did what he told me, fearing what would happen with him being so mad. He might kick my ass, too.

I wished that he would just leave her alone. Helen pulled out a knife to cut him and somehow ended up cutting her own finger. She dripped blood on the floor. I told Smooth to take her into the bathroom and clean her up. He was so angry by this time that he refused to help her. It was her own fault he said, and she could clean herself off. He was determined not to help someone who had no respect for anyone, not even herself.

I helped her into the bathroom and got her cleaned up. I told her it was best if she left right now. Before leaving, she tried to grab Smooth's leg, telling him how much she loved him. I couldn't believe how mad this woman seemed to be over this man, while in reality she was always out there with other men. Her definition of love was very confusing, even for me.

I believed my love for Smooth ran deeper than that even just out of respect for my pimp. I wasn't a woman to sleep around with other men, unless it was about being paid. I respected him, as would another woman in any other relationship. I never talked to another man, even if my man wasn't around. My loyalty didn't stop just because I was out of my man's sight. I had found being disloyal created nasty situations.

After coming back from St. Louis, Mr. Smooth daddy really let himself get hooked on crack. Every day when I came home from work, there he'd be, smoking like a nut with his buddies, puffing my hard-earned, ass-selling dollars away.

I thought to myself, "If I get rid of him, I could smoke the crack all by myself." Sometimes when I smoked with him I thought I had the strength of a bull. No one could tell me what to do after smoking, because it made me feel powerful. It made me think I was King Kong or someone with great power, when in reality it was all just a mind trip. After all, we can't go any higher than where our mind is prepared to take us.

Not long after the kitchen incident, Mr. Smooth informed me he was going to Iowa to pick up Helen and take her back as his other wife. It had been over two years and I thought he was through with her, but money talks and bullshit walks. I asked him why he could even consider taking her back after all the times she had disrespected him. He said it was all about the money. He said we needed the money, especially since he had grown accustomed to smoking up all our money.

I told him that I wouldn't be waiting for him when he came back. Smooth told me that if I weren't there when he returned, he would kill me. I knew I had no choice but to go into hiding.

After Smooth left for Iowa, I called a girlfriend and told her to pick me up. She refused at first because she was afraid of Smooth and what he might do to the both of us.

I told her that he had gone to Iowa and it would take time for him to get there and back. Finally, she was convinced that he was gone and picked me up. As girlfriends, we always came to one another's rescue whenever we needed one another. With just the clothes on my back and a large suitcase of things, I left my belongings all behind and moved back to my old bedroom in Aunt Hazel's house.

After the breakup, I was working at a sauna making lots of money. My new boss never liked pimps and she had helped a lot of girls who wanted to leave their pimps. She told me that I wouldn't have to quit my job at the sauna because of Smooth and that she would help protect me from him. She said I could come to and from work whenever I wanted.

I assumed Mr. Smooth would stop trying to catch up with me as time passed by. I hadn't gone back to the Establishment, or any other bar for that matter, since I split with him. I was too afraid to talk to other black men at this time, fearing they were all pimps. I knew there were white pimps with three and four women out there in the mix of things, as well. Of course, all pimps aren't black, but I feared a black man more than a white man. I knew some of the white pimps who were running around town trying to represent, and they were nothing like the black pimps I knew.

Many of the black pimps were out trying to impress one another by being abusive to their women. These men just wanted women to pay them for their bedroom services. What services, I would wonder. My hand would outlast anyone of those so-called pimps. But when you're working in the fast lane, a lot of women feel as though they needed a man to watch over them. To me this was just a joke, especially when you know they are nowhere in sight when you are taking care of your business. Some chose a man so that another man wouldn't kidnap them.

I had chosen a fast-paced life and to survive I had to learn to play the game better than them. While working at the sauna, I had a special guy I liked who wasn't married. Paul and I liked to talk with each other. He always spent an hour and a half with me, talking a lot of the time. When I told him what had happened with Smooth, he told me he would protect me from my pimp.

After work that evening, I called Paul and he came to my rescue. By now, I had taken enough of Smooth's shit. We went to Paul's apartment and talked until we were tired and then we went to bed together. He told me during the night that he wanted to take care of me.

We woke up together early the next morning. I got up and made us breakfast. Before leaving for work, he handed me a set of keys and told me to make myself at home. It felt good to be with someone who cared about me for who I was.

This man had been paying me to spend time with him twice a week. I knew he dearly wanted to be with me. Shortly after the breakup with Mr. Smooth I started seeing Paul on a regular basis. He would rush home from work each day to be with me. We went out to eat a lot, getting to know one another. I had never dated a white man before I met Paul. He didn't have any children and I was already the mother of four, none of them interracial children.

I wondered what my children would think when I told them I was with a white man. My kids were all sweet children with warm hearts and none of them were prejudiced, so I felt my chances were good.

We decided to pick up all the kids and take them out to eat. While we were out, not one of them even mentioned the fact that Paul was white. He was a very sweet man who liked me—their mother. Everyone seemed to like Paul. We'd go to the movies and professional wrestling matches most weekends with the kids. We all had a good time when we were together. Life was great again for the kids and I.

One day the phone rang at work and it was Mr. Smooth. He had finally caught up with me. I told him that I didn't want to be with him and that I had a new man. He wanted to know who the man was. I told him that it was one of my old clients, that I liked Paul a lot and he was real good to my children and I. He told me that since I didn't disrespect him by getting with another pimp, he would leave me alone. He said I was the only real lady he had met in the profession and that I was too nice for the sauna business. He told me I should move on with my life and that if he had lived a different kind of life, he would never have let me work in the sauna business. He wished me the best.

11

The Best of Both Worlds?

I now had a new life living with Paul. We went to Aunt Hazel's home to explain to her that we wanted to live together. She didn't want to let Rashad leave with me. She and Rashad had spent a lot of time together and she had grown very attached to him. She had taken care of Rashad for about seven years. I wanted Rashad to live with me because he was my son. I knew this would be hard for Auntie to accept, but Rashad was my child and I had a right to keep him with me. I assured her that we would never forget her and that she could spend time with him whenever she wanted.

Finally, she was satisfied that Rashad would still be in her life. I told her what I had been forced to tolerate for three long years with Mr. Smooth. I told her that it was my choice (after being forced at gunpoint) to choose to be with this man, after which I did start having strong feelings for him. The times we spent together were not all bad. We had a lot of great times together as well. I had been afraid to tell her before, because I was afraid that she might try to protect me by attacking Smooth. Just as I thought, she wanted to shoot Mr. Smooth daddy. I knew she was no one to play with. She would have liked to see him squirm like the pig she thought he was.

Paul and I had lived together for about three years now. I was no longer working at the sauna, because he didn't want me to. I wanted to make him happy, so I quit. It didn't feel right to keep working in the sauna after moving in with Paul, anyway.

I didn't mind not working. I felt so much better about myself. Women, including myself, don't necessarily like working in a sauna, but it had provided my children and I with a decent life.

Most weekends Paul would take me shopping and it always made me feel very special. He bought me gold necklaces and ruby or diamond rings. I told him he didn't have to buy me presents all of the time. I told him I didn't want him to get himself into financial trouble. He told me he wasn't spending money he couldn't afford to spend.

One afternoon when Paul came home from work, I told him I didn't feel well and that I had been throwing up all morning. Paul took me to the clinic, where we found out that I was pregnant. Paul was so surprised that he started to cry. He had always wanted to have a child of his own.

We always knew that this could happen, because I wasn't on the pill. Still, it was a bit of a surprise for both of us. We knew we had to tell his mother and that she wouldn't be happy. She thought we were asking for problems, because Paul was white and I was black. His mother felt that our society was not as accepting of interracial relationships as one would hope. We phoned to tell her the news. I admitted that we could have been more careful. Paul's mother told us that it wasn't the child's fault that I became pregnant. She said Paul and I were both adults and we must be ready to accept the consequences of our error. I couldn't believe the way his mother was talking about her soon to be grandchild.

My son's birth was the most satisfying delivery of my life, because I was finally happy with the man I was having a child with. Paul was a very loving and devoted man, and we had a gorgeous little boy. We were shining with pride.

We named him Paul Jr. after his father. He was light-skinned and had a full head of coal black hair. We both adored this new wonder we had helped to give life to. Paul was with me during the delivery. When he cut his son's umbilical cord, he started to cry again. He was so happy. This was his first child. He was thirty-two years old at the time of Paul Jr.'s birth. Paul said he couldn't have asked for a greater gift than the one I had given him.

I breastfed Paul Jr. the first six months. Paul said that I was spending way too much time with the baby and that he was feeling neglected. I asked myself, how could he be jealous of his own child? Some men are so difficult to understand, and I believe that some wish they could take the place of their own children at times. Paul wasn't accustomed to sharing me. He had kept me to himself for quite some time now, and he enjoyed having things that way.

By acting jealously, a man can get most of his wife's attention. Some men just don't seem to understand that parenting takes a lot of time and effort. I didn't want to take care of children all of the time, either. Everyone would like time alone with his or her man, but the baby must always come first.

Men, if you aren't ready for the responsibility, keep your zipper shut or have a vasectomy. That way, you will never have to be responsible for anyone but yourself. Otherwise, get with the program and get real. Life goes on without you, if it must.

When Paul Jr. was about six months old, Paul wanted us to go to Illinois to meet his family. We planned the trip a few months in advance. We rented a new car because our own old Chrysler wasn't reliable enough. I always thought that we would be left stranded alongside the road one day if we drove it.

Paul's family lived on a farm with cows and lots of cats. After arriving at their home in Illinois, I found out that there wasn't any heat upstairs. It was winter and I nearly froze. I couldn't believe that in these modern times they hadn't vented the heat upstairs to the room we slept in. There just didn't seem to be enough covers to keep the baby and myself warm. This didn't seem to bother Paul; he had been raised in that house.

Paul didn't think his family would understand that he had chosen to be with a woman who had been previously married. It was the fact that I had children from my previous marriage that worried Paul the most. Paul believed his mother would think that what had happened in previous relationship's would happen with him and I, as well. This seemed odd to me. I couldn't believe the way this man thought, but looking back at the way his mother acted about me being pregnant, I suppose it was understandable.

Paul's mother was actually very sweet and charming, yet I could tell she had her reservations about me. She, like most mothers, was curious about who her son had chosen. She told me I was a very pretty lady and that we should be proud of our beautiful son. If she felt anger any longer about the pregnancy, she had lost it before we arrived at the farm. She was very nice to me, and treated our son as though he was another one of her grandsons.

Paul's grandmother was a very special lady. She was kind of frail because she was very old. She told me how proud she was that her grandson had found someone he really loved. She didn't see color. That seemed unusual for me, because she was from an older generation than his mother. Growing up when she did, she could have been racist, but she was different than many of the whites I had met when I lived in the South as a child. She was very sweet and loving from the first moment I met her.

Paul and his family always spent holidays together. For several years we spent Christmas out of town with his family. I would spend Christmas with my other children a few days before Christmas in Minnesota, then we would leave town and spend Christmas Eve and Christmas Day with Paul's family down on the farm. I didn't like catering solely to his family on the holidays, because I had kids back in Minnesota with whom I wasn't able to be with. Previous to marrying Paul, I had always spent Christmas together with my children in Minneapolis.

Whenever we went for a visit, he would spend most of his time with his older brother and his sister. He had two other younger brothers who were treated differently by the rest of the family, because they had a different father. I wondered how children could be raised together as a family, and not really be bonded as a family. Some parents allow their children to act differently towards one another. Paul's mother had let him get away with treating two of his brothers differently, because they had different fathers. I was brought up to treat all of my brothers and sisters equally, whether we had the same father or not. We all need to stand up for one another, because this can be a cruel world we live in.

I began to believe that Paul was jealous of his own child. He wasn't handling the change well. I had many sleepless nights, because I wasn't at ease with things anymore. I prayed to God for guidance on whether Paul was the right person for me. I needed to find direction in my life. For some reason, I had begun to feel used and abused but I didn't really understand why.

By this time I had been with Paul about eight years. I assumed he loved me as much as I love him. Over the years, Paul had become like a stranger to me. I didn't know if he was seeing anyone else or not, but I noticed his habits had changed. When our man's habits change, it should put us in the alert mode and we should watch for the red flags.

A woman knows that when her man's habits change, it's time to check him out or have him checked out. Guys give themselves away by being evasive around certain matters. Suddenly he'll leave to run errands, when previously we could never get his lazy butt to move from in front of the television. Now, all of a sudden, he can't wait to go to the store. Guys, slow down, relax, and maybe we wouldn't catch you screwing up. Unfortunately, the majority of you guys will continue to do the same things over and over again expecting a different outcome.

One day, Paul suddenly announced that he was going to Hawaii with his friend, Harry, some man he had never even brought home. Right. And I am

Eddie Quack Quack. I don't think so. Does this man think that I am just a fool or that I was born yesterday? I wasn't the fool my husband thought I was. I was tired of the charade and thought that he could go to hell and back if he wanted to. There comes a time when you get tired of having to check behind your man to see if he is up to no good. He went to Hawaii to stay with his sister at her condo, but I knew he was out messing around.

The past habits of the men in my life had taught me that I should start preparing myself for the coming end. My relationship with Paul was on shaky ground. I didn't know what to do or whom to turn to, because I had totally devoted my life to loving Paul and taking care of my children. They had always come first in my life. They were the reason I was able to continue going on, working against the odds of a life filled with self-destruction. I wondered what I would do if he ever left my children and I. Who would take care of us then?

I hadn't worked for about eight years, not since Paul had insisted he would take care of us. He wanted me to stay at home and raise our son, along with my other kids on the weekends. Feeling like I had to kiss his ass all of the time, I had became a doormat without a voice.

I just got tired of the rat race. Paul had gotten to a point in his life where he really wasn't taking care of himself anymore. His boss had complained to him about his hair not being well groomed anymore.

We both were getting tired of the way our relationship was going. There were so many things that had changed during the course of our relationship. I had finally grown tired of living without a voice. My feelings mattered, too. Who had given him the right to treat me this way? I hadn't done anything but love him with all my heart. We never seemed to have anything to say to one another anymore, not unless we were fighting.

After being with Paul for so long, I knew his habits—and they were changing drastically. Paul used to take me out to eat and other things together, especially when we first got together. Not anymore. He started taking trips alone, without asking me to accompany him. I started preparing myself for the break-up.

I tried to examine our relationship, to put my finger on where it could have gone wrong. We had a dubious start: I was a woman of the night with a straight man (or so I thought). Ironically, I considered Paul a straight man, but I met him while working in a sauna.

It was a mystery to me who was making my man stray. I never let Paul know of my suspicions, I buried them deep down inside, because I was good at suppressing my feelings. As time went on, I thought Paul had given up stepping outside our relationship and things seemed normal again between he and I, so I just let bygones be bygones.

Paul and I even began talking about buying our own house. We found a great location, but the homes were out of our price range, so we hired a realtor to help us find the perfect lot. Once we found a lot, we talked to a contractor about building our little home.

Neither of us had ever owned a home, so this was very exciting for us. We were moving to Savage, Minnesota, a developing suburb that was populated primarily by white people. I didn't know how the neighbors would take to us being an interracial couple, but while our home was being built our neighbors showed us nothing but kindness. Some of them baked cookies and brought them over to us. A few other neighbors took me (a stranger to them) into their homes and showed me how to pick light fixtures and other details. Life seemed to be good for Paul and the rest of us again.

Paul and I had been required to get married as a requirement for purchasing our home. At the ceremony, our realtor was our best man. We got married at the courthouse in downtown Minneapolis by the Justice of Peace.

Near the completion of our home, Paul and I found out my ex-husband's second wife was filing for a divorce. He was still screwing every woman who would let him between her legs. This was nothing new to me, because he had done the same thing when I was married to him. When I was with Tony, I had endured life because I felt safe in that little sick space I had enclosed myself within. Many times I had to forget about my feelings to ensure my children had a roof over their heads and they were safe and secure.

I wouldn't let him have custody of my children without my ex's wife in the picture. I knew he was not the type of man who would be responsible enough to take good care of our children. The only reason I had let him share custody before was because I knew she was stable enough to handle them.

I didn't feel I had any other choice but to get my children from him and bring them to live with Paul and I. I told Paul that he had a choice: He could bow out of our relationship right then or stay with us. He said that he loved me and wanted us to stay together and raise my children along with our son. I told him I would understand if he felt this was too much of a burden to put on him. He told me he was in the relationship for better or worst, as he had stated during our wedding vows.

The six of us were one big, happy family. Our circle was full and we were living a normal life … at least I thought it was normal. Every morning I would get up at the crack of dawn and make breakfast before Paul went to work and the children went to school. I would iron all of their clothes and lay them out. After I saw them all off, I'd think to myself how nice it was to have the house all to myself.

The first three months after the house had been built our home was shown as a model home. The builder had given us the house for $104,000 instead of the original $109,000, so he could show other people the first home built in that particular style. During this time, I was after the kids and Paul to be neat and not mess things up. I ended up doing all the cleaning up after everyone. It brought back such old memories. Memories I just wanted to forget.

Things were eating me up inside from my past. Things I couldn't seem to shake loose. I could barely continue to function at a "normal" capacity. I never really knew what normal was, because no one had ever taught me it. I only knew that I felt that day after day, I was functioning but not living. I didn't know what to feel. I kept all my hurts inside with no one to share them with. "I'm still being a good mother, that's what counts the most," I kept reaffirming to myself over and over.

12

Aunt Hazel

Eventually, I got tired of staying in the house waiting for everyone to get home so that I could serve dinner. I started having Paul drop me off at Aunt Hazel's house on his way to work in the morning. I'd visit with Aunt Hazel until it was time for the kids to get home from school. Paul would pick me up after work and bring me home to make dinner. He started complaining about having to bring me to Aunt Hazel's. He didn't want me to do anything but stay in the house and wait for him and the kids to get home from school, and cook and clean.

I needed to learn how to drive before I went stir crazy staying at home all of the time. I felt so isolated and out of the mix of things. Ladies, if you ever decide to move to the suburbs, you had better make sure you know how to drive. I needed a friend to teach me how to drive, so I called an old customer named Johnny. I knew that Paul wouldn't agree to pay the money it cost for me to go to driving school.

I asked Johnny to teach me how to drive, so I wouldn't be a prisoner in my own home. We would go on a driving lesson and then he would take me out to eat afterwards. I began to feel alive again. Johnny told me how beautiful I was and that I deserved to be in a better relationship. When he said things like this, it made me feel special, because I knew I didn't have to let him touch me to be my friend. I wasn't having an affair with Johnny. I never messed around on my husband, because I believed in being faithful and I still thought I was satisfied with our relationship most of the time.

After weeks of training, I was finally ready to take the test. My girlfriend, Rita, took me to Chaska to take the driving test and I got my license! I felt so proud, like I was among the living rather than the walking dead. No longer was I just a doormat to be trampled upon by my children and my husband. Now I was free to come and go as I damn well pleased and Paul couldn't stop me.

Paul wanted to know how I learned to drive and, of course, I had to tell a lie. I said my girlfriend taught me. I knew that Paul would be highly upset if I told him that I had another man teach me how to drive. I told Paul that Rita thought I needed my driving license to be able to get around, especially if an emergency came up and I needed to take one of the kids to the hospital or doctor. Paul was so angry he didn't speak to Rita for several weeks. Rita didn't know why he was so mad at her. When I told her what I had said in her name, she thought it was so comical. She couldn't believe that he needed to control me in order to be happy himself.

Visiting friends was always one of my favorite pastimes, especially after getting my license. Aunt Hazel's phone call one beautiful morning was a godsend. That morning I didn't have anything in particular to do, so when she called to ask me if I would take her to the hospital to have a radiology test done, I said, "Sure, I'll be right over." She said it wouldn't take more than an hour and a half.

Aunt Hazel was a very strong lady. No one ever crossed her path the wrong way, at least not knowingly. She was not one to take anything off of, by male or female. She was about five feet tall and only weighed 100 pounds soaking wet, but she could have a very bad temper, the bite of a rattlesnake and the sting of a wasp. I adored her. She knew all about my life. There was anything we couldn't talk about. I loved this lady with every ounce of my being. She had always been there for my children and I.

She had been the first person I trusted with my children. She was like a second mother to my son, Rashad. I had grown up with so much hurt and humiliation in my life, because of all my childhood traumas that I was always craving to be loved and recognized. Auntie treated me like I was her daughter. She never had any children of her own.

I was waiting outside the radiology unit at the hospital for Aunt Hazel to get finished with her test when a doctor rushed out of radiology and told me that a doctor had inserted a balloon three times the size he should have into her esophagus. That doctor was fired on the spot, but the damage had already been done to

Hazel. The balloon had split open her chest cavity, and she needed to be operated on right away. I was traumatized by his words and was at a loss.

I called Aunt Hazel's sisters to meet me at the hospital emergency room. I knew I had to get a hold of myself, but at that very same moment I felt a part of me had died. Aunt Hazel's life was in the hand of the Lord and the doctors.

The family had started to arrive one by one and two by two. We sat waiting eight long hours until the surgery was over. The doctors said that Aunt Hazel was in critical but stable condition. I wasn't quite sure what that meant.

The doctors never told us that Aunt Hazel would never be the same again, or that she would just fade away after this day was over. Aunt Hazel never spoke again. She went into a vegetative state. As time went on, we waited for Aunt Hazel to speak or act somewhat normal, but it never happened, not even once. She stayed in the hospital for weeks and never recognized any of us again.

I had lost the most important woman in my life, besides my real mom, who had died when I was only eleven years old. What was I going to do now, I asked myself. I truly had no clue whatsoever.

We took Aunt Hazel to her sister's house after she was released from the hospital. She tried to talk but nothing came out. It was as though they had destroyed her voice box. I was furious about what was going on with her. No investigation was ever conducted to find out really what had happened that horrible afternoon. It still hurts me inside to think about it.

I felt I didn't have anyone to I cry out to. Aunt Hazel had not been an aunt by blood; she was my aunt by adoption and in wishing. I wasn't her sister or her daughter; she had adopted me in her heart because she was a friend who had grown close to my children and me. At times while she was sick, I would talk to her and say, "Auntie, if only I could tell you how much I really adore you." I wish now that I could. I had always said I love you Auntie, but never told how her much she really meant to my children and me. Tell the ones you love how very much you love them. Who knows what tomorrow has to offer? Tomorrow is not promised to any of us. Live today as if there will be no tomorrow, and then perhaps you will say everything you want to all those you love.

I wanted her to get well enough to talk to me one last time. It never happened. I had to feed her, help her sit up, help her use the bathroom. Because she had lost so much of the quality of life, she lost the desire to go on. I wished that I were a doctor so I might have a chance to save her. I prayed that God would give her a voice, so she could speak to me one last time.

A hospice nurse came by twice a week to check on her. This didn't make any difference in her recovery. I knew it was time to start accepting the fact that I would soon lose Aunt Hazel.

She had a needle in her neck for intravenous feeding, and I had to clear the passage by flushing it out daily. Her sister didn't have the stomach to do this unpleasant task, so I was chosen to do it for her. Everyone knew I would do whatever was necessary to prolong Auntie's life. By having to do this painful process, it brought back memories of my mother's death so many years ago.

While Aunt Hazel was so ill, I told my husband that I had to spend as much time with her as possible. He said he understood and knew my grief was deep.

Rashad was only six years old at the time that Aunt Hazel got sick. I started preparing him for the worse. I told him Aunt Hazel may not make it and that we should try to say good-bye. This seemed too much to ask of us, yet deep in our hearts we had to accept the inevitable. Knowing that Auntie was not really living anymore made things a little easier to accept, I didn't wish to see her suffering any longer.

Losing her for good was one of the greatest struggles of my life. After Aunt Hazel's death I couldn't eat or sleep. I didn't want to even talk to anyone. I had previously smoked pot and a little crack here and there, but those desires left me on the day of her death. Even the thought of smoking a cigarette didn't have a place in my life any longer. I had smoked since I was a small child living in Tennessee, since I was four years old, lighting my mother's cigarettes for her.

The time came to start making funeral arrangements—and learning how to say goodbye one last time. On the morning of the funeral, we were all getting ready to go to the church and I decided that it would not be right to have Rashad attend the funeral. I felt he was too young too deal with this situation. We left him with some family members who stayed behind to receive guests after the funeral. I was trying to protect Rashad from being hurt anymore than he already was over Auntie's death.

My girlfriend, who rescued me from Mr. Smooth, was there again for me during another crisis in my life. She came to help receive, cook for and wait on family members and guests at the house after the funeral.

In my eulogy to Aunt Hazel, I tried to sum up what my friendship with her had meant to me by speaking about the times we had shared together—the good times, as well as the trying times. Together we had weathered the storms. I told everyone she was like a mother to me, and no one could ever take her place in my heart. It was time to say good-bye and I couldn't bring myself to say the words. I kept asking myself why I couldn't say good-bye. I think I couldn't let go, because

I had built up so much anger: Anger at the doctors and nurses for sucking the life out of my best friend.

I couldn't bring myself to watch her casket being lowered into the grave, it was too much to bear. My knees were trembling, my teeth were chattering and there was an aching in my heart. I had to leave and wait in the car. To this day, years later, I haven't been able to visit her grave. I think it would bring a closure to our love for one another. I knew I needed help dealing with my grief. That time would arrive some day....

The hospital and staff had gotten away with murder without being charged. I wanted to do something about it, but I had no legal grounds to sue, because I wasn't blood-related. Where was justice when I needed it, I'd ask myself.

I was so devastated that all I could do was grieve. I couldn't function. Aunt Hazel's death had been out of my control. There were times I would open a window, because I felt like I couldn't breathe. I couldn't seem to get enough air. I began having these episodes frequently and I decided it was time to see a doctor to find out what was happening to me.

After the doctor and I talked for a while, he prescribed 2.5 milligrams of Zantex. He told me they would make me feel much better. When Paul brought me home after the doctor appointment, I took one of the pills and slept for thirty-six hours. The following day when I woke up, we called the doctor and told him what had happened. He told me to break the pill in half. This time I fell asleep for sixteen hours. We called the doctor again. And can you believe it? He said to break the pill into fourths. I told him to get screwed.

Here I was, once again, left without any real help for my depression. I told myself I didn't need any medicine. When I lived in the country, we never took medicine for being upset, so why start now? In the country we just sat down for a while and got quiet, and before you know it we were feeling better. Country folks believed in the Lord and that he would heal all of our aches and pains. My parents told me the same as a child. This time, for some reason, it wasn't working and I realized I needed a little extra help. I couldn't shake my problem alone because it seemed bigger than I was. I had let the anger burn too deep and the feelings had become embedded in my soul.

I knew finding a therapist I trusted enough to talk to wasn't going to be an easy task. Still I felt I had to find someone to talk with about the things that were eating me up inside. Once I had this identified my mission, I knew it was going to be one of my greatest battles. I believed at the time that it would be a lot easier than it turned out to be.

13

Facing the Music

One day as my daughter and I were driving down the freeway, I felt uncomfortable, but had no idea as to why. I told Shanita not to be alarmed, but I needed to drive to the hospital to see a doctor. She said, "All right mom. I am here with you and I will help take care of you." My children were always there to take care of me, especially because Rashad kept us on our toes with his attention deficit disorder.

When I arrived at the emergency room, I told the doctors about my breathing problems. The doctors ordered an EKG (an electrocardiogram) to make sure there wasn't anything wrong with my heart. Nothing was wrong with my heart, of course. The doctor had me to sit on the bed, and then he asked me to amuse him by jumping off the bed and breathing really fast. After doing this, I asked the doctor for a glass of water. I told him I felt as though I couldn't breathe. He said I was having what was called a panic attack.

I wondered if I was going crazy. I asked the doctor if I was and he said no. He said we needed to find out what was causing me to feel that way. He referred me to the Medicine Clinic at County Medical Center.

At the Medicine Clinic, I told the doctor I thought I was going crazy. The staff informed me that millions of people after the age of thirty sometimes have these kinds of problems, especially when they have several kids to care for.

I was under a lot of stress. What the doctor didn't know was that black folks don't typically believe in letting family members know we might have "those kind of issues," such as depression or mental illness. Denial and stuffing is what so many of us have done as a way of taking care of ourselves, especially when we don't know what else to do.

I thought people who lost control of their emotions, like I felt I had, needed to be institutionalized. Pills weren't going to help me. I wondered why I felt this way. Could it be because my husband and my children were driving me crazy? Was this the reason I was so stressed out?

Being a mother most of my life without any real training had been very draining, enough to drive even the strongest person a bit crazy. Always being in control of my emotions took a lot of patience. Patience doesn't come without a lot of practice, something I didn't feel I had time to master. By this time in my life, I felt all practiced out and my energy level had been diminished.

And what book has all of the answers for being a responsible parent? None to my knowledge. The only knowledge I had to use was that I had learned along the way from my parents. My mother had died at such an early age and my stepmother never had the time or inclination to teach me anything except feelings of being unloved and unwanted. Who was to tell me when I didn't have the answers to all of my children's questions? I didn't feel that there was anyone for me to ask for advice on all of my problems and pains. I had no one to confide in, so I continued to keep my feelings within myself. This was the core of my problem, something I began to realize during my therapy sessions.

The healing process was a long, hard road for me. The Medicine Clinic had scheduled me to attend sessions with a therapist. My first therapist's office was in Burnsville, a neighboring suburb. The first thing my therapist, Denita, wanted me to do was to go all the way back to my childhood, so she could analyze where my problems came from. I didn't want to go there with her because the road felt too painful to travel. I began to shut her out right away. I thought, "Why should I trust her?" Coming from Tennessee (a racist state) and then growing up in Indiana (another state where blacks and whites didn't get along), made me instantly suspicious.

I was married to a white man and I thought this white woman would try to tell me I needed to leave my husband. I thought she figured no black woman needed to be with a white man anyway. So, naturally, I wasn't going to take Denita's advice—at least not in the state of mind I was in at the time.

And, anyway, who wants to go back to all the hurt and pain that had been locked away for so long? I asked myself, why should I tell a stranger how hard the road was that I had traveled? Denita assured me that things sometimes seem painful because we hold onto them for so long that they can make us sick. Sick, I thought. Lady, if you only knew what sick really was, you might run out of this room screaming right now. If only you knew what you are asking of me. I wasn't sure I was ready to deliver.

Finally, after seeing Denita for about eight months, I started to tell her about all the incest that had gone on in my past from the age of six through eleven. She wanted to know who had abused me. I told her about my stepbrothers who had raped me on a daily basis. They had hurt me so deeply that talking to her about it made me feel as though I were living it all over again. I told her that I had wanted them to leave me alone, but I was too weak to fight them off. They kept hurting me over and over again.

At some point, I told her, I felt I must have somehow asked for what they were doing to me. Not only that, but I also had begun to feel that it was all right because it helped to cover up the pain of watching my mother being abused. Momma had told me when I was small that I should treat them like real brothers. I knew even then that a real brother wouldn't do what they had done to me; they didn't treat me like a sister. I never had an opportunity to really live as a child—playing and exploring, because I was treated by my stepbrothers like a girlfriend instead of as their sister. I never really trusted boys—and as I got older, men either.

When you've had your childhood sucked away from you, somehow you feel you never had the chance to be normal, especially if you've been treated as an adult most of your life. This feeling that it was always my fault and that I was just not strong enough to fight them off, had caused me to doubt myself throughout life.

I realized in therapy that I was just a child who was afraid that her mother wouldn't understand what had truly happened to me if she knew. I thought as a child that there was no way momma would believe me if I said they had raped me. I believed it was best to be quiet and that it would all just end one day and go away. During the time of the abuse, I had been concerned about the damage that knowing would have done to her health. I didn't want my mom to stop loving me.

Sometimes I didn't know if I had the strength to continue. Denita wanted to put me on antidepressants. Wanting nothing to do with taking pills, I declined. I didn't believe in medication. I believe that medication is often a cover-up and wouldn't truly cure me of my ailments.

My therapist recommended the whole family come in for counseling. Raising five children, four of them boys, had been challenging. Somehow I had managed to take care of all my children better than many families with two children.

The next week I brought all of the children with me to the therapist. She talked with each of them individually. We did weekly visits, which brought out some of the problems that had caused me to become so ill. When I was having a panic attack, I felt weak and felt like I was on the verge of having a nervous breakdown.

I discovered that I was trying to be both a mother and a father to my children. Paul and I were married, but he didn't help tell my children what to do or discipline them. That was supposed to be my job—and my job alone. The only child Paul directed was Paul Jr. We were a family with two sets of rules: one set for my kids and another set for our son together. I had never thought that he was wrong to act this way. I never liked it, but he paid the bills so I thought it was up to me to accept things as he wanted them. That was what I had always done in the past. Between the kids and Paul, I had become a doormat.

As therapy continued, I began to breathe more freely. My therapist said that everyone needed someone to talk to. I hadn't had anyone in my life I considered close enough to talk to since Aunt Hazel's death.

Being with Paul for so many years made me feel that I couldn't trust him to help me feel safe and secure. I disliked Paul hiding things from me and his sneaky ways. I was his wife, but he seemed to treat me like I was just his girlfriend.

My therapist told me she felt that Paul needed help, because of all the secrets he was carrying around. What was I suppose to do? Spank him because he was being naughty. Paul refused to go to therapy, because he said I was the one with the problem and not him. I had talked myself into believing him, so I put up with his crap by turning the other cheek, you might say.

One day I was home not doing much, so I decided to inspect his file cabinet Paul had been locking. When I got it open, I found about thirty pieces of paper with different women's names on them. I wondered all afternoon while he was at work about what the meaning behind them was. When Paul arrived home from work that evening, I was raring to ask him why he had so many women's names in his cabinet. When I questioned him, he told me that I would be mad at him if he told me. When he finally told me what they were, I laughed. Each slip had the name of an adult movie star written on it. I found this amusing. What was wrong with seeing a few adult movies? He was a grown man. Men can be so evasive over such silly things.

I still didn't know my husband was having an affair and spending quite a bit of money on working women. Paul never called what he was doing having an affair. In his mind, he was just paying to have sex with other women. To some men, including Paul, that is not adultery.

We had met at the sauna, but I never even imagined that he would end up seeing other women once we were married. A friend of mine had told me that once a trick always a trick. I had never seen Paul as just an ex-trick.

I didn't mind him watching porn movies, because I thought it was what a lot of men did. I knew he couldn't jump into the TV and bang one of those nude stars. So what damage was being done and what was there for me to be leery of? Men sometimes cause women to be suspicious for no reason whatsoever, because they overreact to our questions. For me, when he told me where the names came from, there was no reason for us to discuss it any further.

I finally woke up when my therapist had asked me if I was the parent who sometimes got up in the morning with the kids and got them ready for school. I said, "You must be kidding. Do I do this sometimes? Try every morning." I always made my children and Paul something to eat and ironed and laid out their clothing for school. I even ironed his t-shirt.

When he complained about how I did the laundry I would say to myself, "Why don't you fold them yourself?" When I told the therapist this, she wanted to know why, if I thought this, didn't I tell him how I felt.

"Because he would be upset with me," I said.

"Aren't you upset when he and the kids expect you to do everything?" she asked.

"That's part of my job as a parent," I told her.

"Why was it your job?" she asked me.

"Because I had a contract," I said. By this I meant that I was the mother of my children and had taken Paul in marriage, and I believed it was my duty to fulfill my end of the bargain.

"I don't feel as though that's true either, so why must it be your job to take care of the man and the children?" she asked again. This made me stop and think hard.

My therapist asked me to ask each of my boys if they appreciated my ironing their clothes. I glady asked of them. And, each one of those little monsters [that's how I felt at the time] one by one told me that they didn't appreciate me ironing their clothes. I couldn't believe my ears. They said that they wanted to go to school with wrinkled clothes like the other kids.

I thought my children and my husband were so unappreciative. Paul thought my therapist was putting her nose where it didn't belong. In reality, she was taking this little ass wipe from the clutches of his controlling hands. He wanted nothing to do with therapy because he didn't think he or the family had a problem. He said that I was the nut of the family and he was the family's brain.

It seemed like all of my life I had lived and worked for the betterment of my children. Paul seemed more and more like a boyfriend as time went on. My therapist told me she thought he controlled me in subtle ways. He had his own checking account and he hid the retirement account records where I couldn't check them. I had no way of knowing what he had put away for our future. Paul didn't tell me much about our financial situation, and I didn't question him. You would have thought he was a millionaire. I had never wanted to take his money. I had tried to show him how much I loved him and not his money.

Some men don't appreciate their wives until they start losing control over them. They don't wish to appear weak in the eyes of their wives—and if they admit they have a problem they think it will make them appear weak. Often when a woman suggests that her man get help with his issues, the man points his finger back in the woman's direction instead of dealing with his problems. These guys need to wake up and smell the roses. The grass isn't greener on the other side. Nothing comes without a price tag attached to it. Those hidden costs will get you in the end. As a woman, I feel many of us give our bodies for money [security] in our relationships. We just don't label it prostitution. When holidays came I expected a present from my husband. That goes for birthdays and anniversaries as well. If he wanted some head, then buy me something big and expensive I would tell him. Some people label me certain ways for thinking that way. I believed this was my way to survive and to give my children most of the things they ever wanted. For some time, I had been suspicious that Paul was having an affair. I had many warning signs, but I ignored most of them.

For the last five years of my marriage to Paul, I felt driven to give my other four children what Paul and his family was only willing to give our youngest son. I still had responsibilities as a parent to my other children. They needed things, too, and I wanted as a mother to be able to provide them those things. I was tired of arguing with Paul to give me money to buy things for my children. No man was going to make me deny my children their needs. I decided to start working at the sauna again.

Life after therapy led to a divorce with Paul. I found out that after all the love I had given him, he was having sex with other women behind my back. At first I was going to just let it go, but I couldn't do that anymore.

I think of all the times in the past when I wondered if he was cheating and how I brushed the red flags under the rug. Now that my mind had become clear I knew why he was hiding the phone bills and locking the file cabinet. He may have been cheating on me the whole time; I had refused to acknowledge the signs.

My love hadn't meant much of anything to the men in my life. They had always been looking for Ms. Right (someone who would kiss their ass). My therapist told me that I probably shouldn't have married Paul. She said my love for him was only gratitude. I found she was right. Love is much deeper than gratitude—it is total satisfaction. First we must search and find our own self, and then we are truly free. The ghosts of our past can no longer haunt us, unless we are a willing source of those memories.

Moving on with my life was not going to be an easy task, but I was ready and stronger than ever before. I found an apartment in Burnsville. I was still working in a sauna making real good money. After being on my own for several months I met a man named Carl. He was much older than I was. I liked older men because they seemed to not run around as much as the younger ones. They've learned that what shows on the outside may not be as pretty on the inside. And they no longer need to explore new horizons, because they realize that those roads have more than likely already been traveled all too many times.

Carl enjoyed buying me everything my heart desired and then some. He gave me the world on a silver platter. He gave me diamonds, rubies, gold and silver. There was never anything I desired that he told me I couldn't have. I didn't love him because he didn't seem strong enough for me. I still believed I needed a man who took control of all situations. I seemed to have a craving for a macho man. What a joke! We think like idiots at times when our minds are fogged by the smooth words of silly men. A lot of us go through life searching for a man who will love us the way we can love them.

Carl couldn't understand why I didn't want to marry him. We went on trips and he gave me all the fancy things that money could buy, but I still couldn't be happy. Throughout my life I had always relied on making my own money and not depending on a man to lead me by my nose. I was never any good at being financially dependent on someone else. I had tried that with Paul and the flavor never seasoned my mouth.

None of the materialistic things ever really mattered to me in a relationship. Love was what I was searching for and never found to be the way I thought it should be. I had a particular idea in my mind as to what true love looked like, but how could I have possibly known what it looked like if I had never felt really loved?

Carl gave me more respect than I could give myself at the time, so why couldn't I love him? I had a feeling deep down inside that God knew who my chosen one was and he was leading me in that direction. I had known since I was eleven years old where my destiny in love would lead me.

My children were at the age where I could see the light at the end of the tunnel in terms of raising them. They were almost all old enough to be on their own. There would soon be no more living for someone else, but living and believing in myself.

Ten years ago, I thought I had found Mr. Right, the man of my dreams: a strong man with a will of iron. Shelly, one of my girlfriends, introduced me to him. She told me he was someone I could trust. She knew about my rocky past with men and that my marriage had fallen apart. She also knew that I was not in love with Carl (he was my sugar daddy).

I had told Shelly that I had tried for a long time to preserve my marriage by showing my husband that I was serious about our love, but he had pushed me farther and farther away.

My eyes were totally open when I was introduced to the one I thought could be Mr. Right. Shelly knew that I didn't care enough to marry Carl, so she introduced me to TJ. From the moment I met TJ at the Mad Mad Mexican Restaurant, I knew he was the one for me. He turned me on from the moment I met him. After our meal was over, I didn't want to let him leave, but I knew it was for the best.

Never let a man know how much you like him on your first date. He's bound to take advantage of the lust you show and see it as a weakness. I had never had such a strong feeling for a man on my first date with him. I felt such a passion burning deep down inside me. I knew he could satisfy my thirst.

While outside saying goodbye, he asked me if he could see me again. I said yes. I gave him my number and told him to give me a call. The next evening he called and asked me out on another date. We went to shoot pool and then we went and rented a room at a hotel. I surprised myself doing this so quickly with him, but I enjoyed every moment of his time.

TJ and I had a very wonderful time together making love passionately all evening long. I have never felt so much love in my life as I did relaxing in his arms. This was strange to me, being a woman who hated having a man sweat on her. His sweat seemed to turn me on even more. All those things didn't matter. All that mattered was that we were together.

After we finished making love, I told him that no man had ever made me feel so deeply. He turned me on just being with him. A feeling that I could love him forever was burning within my soul. I had never really had the opportunity to love anyone so passionately before.

I wanted to spend as much time with him as possible. How could I feel so strongly about someone I hardly even knew? Was it just that I so hungry for love—any love? Or was this truly the real thing? I had been hurt so much throughout my lifetime that it was really hard for me to believe that a man could really love me the way that I could adore and love him. I decided after the initial passion, that I would take it slow with TJ and not rush into another deep mess.

Shelly couldn't believe I was so taken by TJ. I asked her why and then she told me he was a flirtatious asshole. How could she tell me this now? She was the one who had introduced me to this man as someone I could trust. Why did she introduce me to him if he wasn't going to be good for me?

I didn't feel she really knew him as well as she said she did. She said that she thought I would just use him like Carl. I said that I hadn't used Carl, he had just borrowed my services for a while.

TJ couldn't really afford my tastes. I didn't need any money from him anyway, especially since he was what I thought the doctor had ordered. He was someone who could appreciate being loved completely. I felt this was the man for me, though he seemed at times to be stuck on himself, but for some odd reason, I still found myself falling deeper and deeper in love with him.

Shelly was right. TJ was a womanizer. Being a woman of the world with years of experience, I noticed he wasn't to be totally trusted. I decided to ignore the bad behavior. Love them or leave them. After all, most men I had ever had the opportunity of loving had some kind of baggage to bring to the relationship with them, and to me his was not going to be any heavier.

We had been together for about six months or more when he informed me that he had a fifteen-year-old son with another lady who lived in Bloomington, a neighboring suburb. He was always to find a reason to go there for a visit. He kept telling me that she didn't mean anything to him, and she was just someone he had a child with. TJ told me that he loved being with me and wanted to be with me more than anyone else.

What was that supposed to mean? Did I give up everything from my past for another broken promise? Paul had turned out to be dishonest, and I was wondering if I had found that relationship again—another fake lover.

Feeling as though I wasn't completely ready to fall heads over heels with another problem, I decided to take things a little slower. To keep things cool, I'd go out dancing with my girlfriends to have some fun and to meet other men. It didn't matter where I went, he was always on my mind. And even though I met a couple of nice guys, I didn't strike up much interest in being with them.

No matter whom I was with, TJ never left my mind. I asked Shelly why she had introduced me to a man like TJ when she knew he liked to be in the company of different women. She told me that he didn't know what it meant to be in a serious relationship and that commitment was the last thing on his mind. He felt he needed to be free to have sex with whomever he pleased.

TJ knew about my sugar daddy, Carl, and he kept pressuring me to continue seeing him because the payoff was great. He said that seeing Carl wouldn't keep him from caring about me. I should have checked myself at this point. How can a man love a woman he tosses away into another man's arms? I refused to believe that he didn't truly love me as much as I loved him. Unfortunately, just because I had no interest in being with Carl, didn't necessarily mean TJ had no interest in being with other women. There were times that just the sight of Carl made me feel ill. By my continuing to see Carl, TJ didn't have to feel guilty about the wrong he was doing to me. It justified his behavior in his mind.

I had informed Carl many times that I didn't love him, but he insisted that he didn't care that I didn't love him because he really wanted to spend time with me. I continued seeing him because he kept buying me presents, and I loved the fact that someone wanted to wine and dine me, even though I would have preferred that the gifts had come from TJ. My heart ached deeply for TJ to return my feelings, instead he just didn't seem to understand how much I truly loved him.

The other men from my past always showered me with gifts and waited on me hand and foot. That didn't make me want to love them. They had seemed too weak for me. I learned in therapy that this was because of the way I had been abused in my past. I felt that a man must be strong above all things. The men from my past let me do the ruling. I thought I needed a man with a mind of his own.

At that time, I needed an asshole, I guess, to put me in my place and to keep me in check. The type of lifestyle I lived had created a pattern for me. I needed someone who would let me know that I didn't always have to be in control to love someone. Being in control of a situation seemed to be my only defense. Because I had been controlled most of my life, I took control back whenever possible.

TJ always told me he liked to party with the fellows and the girls at the bars. Slut bars, I called them. He took me to a few, and oh man, were they ever sleazy. He seemed to fit right in with the crowd, because at these bars the women were falling all over the men. For the women at the bar, the men weren't within their every day reach. They kept reaching for that impossible dream, as I had at one time in my life.

If TJ had only thought about how easy it was for those sluts to give themselves so freely, he would have ran out of that bar. Those women are the ones men should be hesitant of, because most of them have slept with quite a few men without even a thought of catching or passing on a disease. These women who call themselves "ladies" are no more than prostitutes who aren't getting paid for their services. I would much rather be paid for the services I provide to a man. At least I know they wouldn't brag about what he did with me to his buddies. Usually men who visit a sauna for services don't run around telling their buddies that they've paid a woman for sex.

To these sluts of the night, I was just a whore. But this whore took care of her children and didn't have to live waiting on a monthly welfare check. At least I always knew where my condoms were. Many of these women are too drunk when they give out to even worry about a condom. Don't they not know that AIDS is an epidemic?

I only found this out about TJ after we had been together for a while and I thought I was in love with him. Had I known it before getting more involved with him, I might have made a different choice in selecting to get serious with him.

It took TJ a long time to let go of some of the women from his past, but as he got older, he slowed down his pace. Women were always paging him, trying to beg for his attention. For some reason, men seem to take longer to let go of the excess baggage from their past. They never seem to realize that what they have, until it is almost too late for them to keep what's best for them.

Each time after a night at the bars, he would come home and I would tell him to take his clothes and get the hell out of my life because I was better off without him hurting me. He would promise things would get better and, once again, I would forgive him. A man usually knows when you mean what you say and when you are just threatening him to get him to fly right. So, ladies, if you don't plan on leaving him, don't make idle threats. It won't make him straighten up or change his bad habits.

No matter how many times I asked him to leave, he never left. TJ would ignore me, take off his clothes and go to bed. When we'd wake up in the morning, it would be as though nothing had ever gone wrong. Why, I'd ask myself, should I let him get away with this type of behavior? Never coming up with an answer, I just kept forgiving him and letting him do what he had always done. That is why I knew that I must love this man, because I hadn't taken this kind of behavior from any man since my first husband—and that was because I didn't know any better.

Every six months I would go to the doctor and have all of the STD (sexually transmitted disease) tests run, but they were always negative. I was afraid to trust him.

TJ told me the two women who couldn't seem to quit calling him (one being his ex-girlfriend) meant nothing to him. Often I would find numbers on his phone that he couldn't explain, and he would tell me it was none of my business whose numbers they were. If a woman doesn't mean anything to a man, then why does he keep talking to her?

TJ's kids were almost grown and could call their father if they wanted or needed to talk with him. It didn't take his ex to make sure he spoke with them.

One day I said to TJ, "Maybe I should call these friends of yours and see why they keep calling you. Maybe they might have something different to share with me."

He didn't respond to me about this situation. He didn't know I had his security code to check the calls coming into his pager. I wondered why he hadn't responded. It seemed as though the cat had gotten his tongue.

I told TJ, "Maybe I need to call the number she leaves since she only phones on Sundays, because her man must be working or out of the house. Maybe I need to call the line and speak to the man of the house and see what he thinks about this particular situation I am dealing with." I told TJ that there was no way that he could expect me to believe anything he told me about this woman because her number was always on his pager.

I will slice and dice me a big chunk of his cock to feed to his slut, I told him. I thought that maybe he wouldn't want to accept her pages anymore after hearing those words. I thought maybe I should move on with my life and never trust another man again. Men can be dogs at times. If a man loves the woman he's with, there shouldn't be a need for another woman to call him. How would they feel if the situation were reversed?

I wanted a man who could give me the same respect that I showed him, and if he couldn't return the respect, then I would prefer to be single.

I said to TJ, "If you aren't happy with me, then move on with your life. There's no need to keep me guessing, there are too many free people out there for each of us to hook up with. I can be miserable alone. I don't need anyone helping put me in this frame of mind."

"Baby," I said, "I can't give you anymore love than I already have, so you had better change your sly ways or move on to the next phase of your life."

"I know you have never been married," I said, "but if you want to really be in a serious relationship, you had better change your sneaky ways."

"I didn't ask to fall so deeply in love with you," I continued. "It is something that happened to both of us. You tell me you still love me the same. Start showing it or I will leave you."

"Your days of running around are over," I told TJ.

This time I had opened my heart wide open. True love just happens and nothing we try to do to stop these feelings seems to stop them. TJ knew I was tired of playing games with him and he needed to get serious. This was the first time in my life I really felt totally free and in control of my life. I had been through the wimps, the simps and the pimps—some of whom had been considered the best in that profession.

"I know you have changed so much to try to keep this relationship going," I said, "and I feel you have done these things for a reason, but I need one hundred percent because that is what I have given to you. My eyes see no other man but you, my darling."

"You have wandering eyes, for what, I am not sure," I said. "You say your search was over when you found me, but I am not here for the duration just to receive lip service. Words said without substance void their meaning and I need substance to feel loved."

"When a man roams the streets after 12:30 a.m. there is nothing out there open but legs and whores. If I am what you want and I am giving you all the nourishment you can handle, then baby, let me have your eyes and your heart because I could not give you any more of mine, there would not be any left for me to survive."

"You have given me the kind of support I have needed to weather the storms. If you are planning to just walk out the door and never turn back, take a second look. Life will go on in time for me, it always has in the past and it will again," I said.

TJ knew if anyone picked me up and dated me, my stuff wasn't free. Those men would have to pay handsomely for my time. I hadn't slept with many who hadn't had to pay for my troubles. I still had five mouths to feed when I confronted TJ. He informed me that he understood my situation and where I was coming from.

TJ knew that I always used protection when I was working and had never given him anything. I was tested regularly for HIV/AIDS, syphilis, and gonorrhea etc. I wasn't getting tested because I went without protection, but as a safety precaution.

A working woman is very devoted to her man, unless she is ready to choose a replacement. Some women are sluts no matter how good their man is to them, because some are just born to be nymphomaniacs. She doesn't make it a habit of giving sex to anyone for free—she must get paid. Money is what makes her world go-round. A freebie for anyone is the last thing that would probably happen. When approached for a freebie, I told most men where they could get off and how quick.

TJ had no interest in being a pimp because he had been down that road in the past and it wasn't worth the headaches that came along with playing that role. He worked at a job, so could make his own money and not rely on a woman.

Slowly, TJ decided to reform his wayward ways. He quit going to the bars and chasing after other women. And after five years together, TJ and I were wed. We call this the "final closure." TJ and I decided together that we were ready to be totally committed when we took the plunge. We already knew a lot of what was in store for us and we were ready to love each other to the fullest. Our days of bullshitting each other were finally over, no more running the streets looking for someone else to fulfill our lusty desires. Flesh is a human weakness, and I believed we must learn to live in the spirit and not the flesh.

TJ finally knew that if he wanted to be with other women it was best not to marry me, because I am not the one to be played with. He knows if he gets caught playing around I will have to play hardball. I will leave him or play the game a little harder than he can. So, ladies, warn them before they take the plunge, because there is always another direction they can follow. If a man wants to play the field, it is best he never marry. Otherwise, he'll pay the consequences for getting caught stepping out on the wrong woman.

TJ and I found our final destination: total devotion to one other. The running around part of our lives was behind us and we were pressing on towards a better tomorrow. Money was no longer the root of our evil. Our children were well taken care of and the door to our new life was open.

I was still going to therapy periodically. My therapist told me that in order to feel whole, I needed to close the door to the ghosts of my past and move on with my life. She said I had been trying to heal a deep wound with just Band-aids, when really I needed stitches. I thought the Band-Aids could hold me together, that is until I came up against a crooked system.

14

The Dirty Bust

During my work at the sauna, I had always had problems finding peace with my feelings about the work I did. My work and my Christian beliefs were always in conflict with one another. Battling one's self is the most difficult enemy, because the entire time we are "working" we are struggling for salvation. I have never felt shamed by other people about what I did to feed and clothe my children. My work kept me off of the welfare system for many years and for that I am proud, but it was time to move on. I had always believed that if a person is capable of working, then he or she should work—no matter what that work is. If I had a mental illness or was illiterate that would be different, but I am not illiterate, blind or insane. I knew that I had to figure out why I engaged in self-destructive behavior.

I needed forgiveness only in the eyes of my Lord. I wanted to get to heaven and see my mother again, so I decided I needed to press ahead to win my salvation by focusing on a new beginning.

My therapist told me that she felt that I didn't need much more therapy. She didn't know that I was working at the sauna. I hadn't fully opened up to her—or myself—at this point.

At this time, I thought I was happier than I had ever been: TJ and I were getting our life together and I was finding closure to my dark past and my profession as a call girl once and for all. Finally, I could breathe again and I felt like a whole person. The only thing I still needed to do was to end my profession, and I was well on my way to doing that. I was forty-four years old and I felt stable because of eight years of therapy. My panic attacks were almost gone and I could feel myself becoming stronger inside each day. But before I could end it on my own, the system robbed me of that closure.

At the sauna over the years I had massaged a number of police officers. I usually gave them a massage or let them massage me and tell them when their massage was finished. In fact, a police officer told me when I first starting working at a sauna that as long as I didn't greedy, I would never get busted. This was a useful piece of advice I had always kept in my mind.

I have never had a desire to get greedy. My marriage with Paul had lasted for fourteen years, and I had worked the last three years of that marriage. I got tired of begging my husband for money to spend on my kids' clothes. By this time we were married in name only, anyway. I had been granted my divorce in February 1997, and knew I had money coming from my divorce settlement. I had known for months, so I knew I didn't need to be greedy. To me, greed was an even greater sin in the eyes of God, because to me my work was a necessity of survival and greed was excess.

At the sauna, we were a group of working girls who had grandma from next door coming over to have a cup of coffee. At Christmas, the rest of the ladies and I gave her and another neighbor a hundred dollars for presents. When Grand Forks, North Dakota, was flooded in 1997, we got together and sent them five hundred dollars to help with their relief effort. It was our way of showing our support—even for those who may not support us.

On several occasions the police had been harassing customers leaving the sauna. They would ask the customers all kinds of questions regarding the girls. They told customers they had already busted one of our girls for attempted prostitution. Actually, she really hadn't had sex with an officer.

I am not here to speak for her or any other incident, I am reliving this nightmare over and over in my heart and mind. It cost me a great deal more than just money. On the evening of July 15, 1997, I had been at work for several hours when the girls and I felt things seemed strange. There hadn't been any customers.

Not one of the three of us had given a massage this particular evening. This is because police officers were outside the door.

When the doorbell rang and I saw who was at the door, I told the other two girls that he looked like an officer. My instincts told me to proceed with caution. It was an assumption until I checked him out. When I opened the door I asked if he had been here before. He said yes about eight months ago.

I asked him whom he had seen. He said Jennifer. To me, Jennifer was a "bad" name. Working women have "good" and "bad" name as a way of protecting ourselves by identifying the good guys from the bad ones. I offered him his choice of girls and he chose me to give him a massage. He said that because I had answered the door, he would be fine with me massaging him. I showed him to a room at the front and told him the massage was forty dollars.

Giving a massage was my only "sin" on the day in question. I always knew taking chances might mean I could end up going to jail. When a man came in for sex, I knew right away he was there for more than a massage. Police officers go through the motions, but they never really relax. They are too tense to be at ease. Men who visit saunas come for more than a massage and act accordingly right away. They know what it takes to get serviced. I knew where to draw the line even before the game began with the officer.

In the past, whenever I had given a police officer a massage, he hadn't violated me. I'd give him a massage and send him on his way. I could always tell whether an officer was trying to entrap me, he stood out like a sore thumb. There are certain boundaries that officers won't cross. I didn't do anything wrong, so I believed he would follow the book and be on his way, but not this one. He would rather fake a dirty bust.

I asked him if he would like to take a shower before his massage. He said no. I left the room to give him time to undress. I wondered why he had chosen to see me. It could have been because he assumed that all black girls have previous records for prostituting.

I gave him some water and showed him where the towels were for him to cover himself. I told him I would be right back. I went to inform the other girls that I was just going to give him a massage and let him go because I didn't trust him enough to do anything else. I had learned that when I had a gut instinct, I had to go with it. This is what had kept me safe all those years. I never changed my mind after making a decision based on instinct. This had always been my motto and I never swayed from it.

From the beginning to the end, I had planned on nothing more for him than a plain and simple massage. I told him before I started that I would massage his chest, back and legs and arms—nothing more and nothing less. He said that would be fine. During the massage he and I made a lot of small talk. There was no sexual conversation. I massaged him for about a half an hour and then told him his massage was finished. He asked me if he could get some more massaging. I said he could massage me for a half an hour the same way that I had massaged him or have me massage him again for another forty dollars. He chose to massage me.

I was wearing a nice blue dress, so I excused myself to change into a bathing suit. My clothes were too expensive to get oil all over them. He started to massage me, and as time passed by he asked if he could massage my breasts. I said, "No, you may not." He continued massaging me and eventually asked if he could lift my bathing suit and I said no you may not, again.

Finally I told him his time massaging me was over. He then asked me if he could massage my clitoris. I angrily said no, once again. As I was about to get up from the bed, he looked at me and he said in a loud voice, "Where's the condom?" and "Can I lick you?" I told him that he may not lick me and what did he need a condom for?

At this point I began to feel as though I was about to be raped. The massage had gone fine, but the officer continued to be very pushy and that is definitely a no-no in my line of business. After I informed him that his massage was over for the second time and it was time for him to leave, I heard a loud banging on the door. I looked at the customer and asked him what was going on outside. He acted stunned. He said that he didn't know what the noise was and that he didn't hear a thing.

I should've known he was full of baloney. When I got out of the room into the hallway, I looked at the front door of the sauna. The officers had broken down the door to get in. The officer I had given a massage to was still in the front room. He finally came out and told the other officers that I was the one under arrest for prostitution. I looked at the other officers and asked "What prostitution? There's no prostitution going on here."

He asked me if that's the way I saw it. I said yes, I couldn't see it any other way. The next thing I knew, I was handcuffed and told to sit down on the couch. I was wondering what in the hell was going on. Life is a bitch when you are a black woman in my profession, I was thinking. Not only did I have to suppress the shame of my work, but I had to go through crap like this.

Later, I asked another officer if it was because of the new "nuisance law" that they were harassing me. He said yes, and that they used the nuisance law because it was too difficult to bust girls for prostitution alone. At least when I asked the other officer about the nuisance law, he was honest. Not all police officers are bad people, they have a job to do and they do it right sometimes. But working with a bad cop will make even the best cop hesitate to do the right thing in situations on the job.

Some may believe that because of the type of work that I did that I shouldn't be treated fairly in the justice system, but I still had rights and there are laws that must be followed—even by officers. I was to find out that this officer had no limits to his dirty ways, which made me even more resistant. He had a job to do as well as I did. I did my job, but he lost sight of his when he couldn't get a clean bust.

He forgot he had to follow the law by the book. What he didn't realize is that a book of law was built within my mind. I knew the limits and the lines. I had learned the tricks of the trade very well. Evidently, the officer's memory had lapsed so badly that he no longer understood what the word of law meant. The law didn't give this officer or any other officer the right to misuse his badge or his authority. How can we teach our children to obey laws that violate others rights as though they had none?

Can the system take away our rights for its own benefit? I had to pay an attorney money that I didn't have for the convenience of the system. I felt like I was the one violated. I had to spend four days in court. For what? To be humiliated?

The officer didn't have any consequences to suffer. I showed up for court every day as asked. If I hadn't, I would have had to pay an even higher price. Being at court was the hardest thing I had ever been through in my adult life. It was so humiliating, even turning tricks left me with more dignity. In court, I sat before a panel of jurors who didn't know the first thing about who I truly was. They were judging me for a wrong I hadn't even been caught committing.

The day that I had my say in court the arresting officer chose not to show up, even though I had been humiliated in front of the jurors with tears running down my face every time the officer told his false side of what happened. The court clerk said he was sick, but if I had been sick I would have been considered guilty automatically. He lied so he didn't have to show up for the final day in court. It was already over for him and his lying ways. On top of that, he didn't have to spend a dime for court costs or lost work time.

Where was my justice? I guess I had none. My friends told me I should be happy because it was over. Happy for what I would like to know. I am the one who had to disclose to my twenty-two year old son, Teddie, that I might be charged falsely for soliciting an officer. My son never had any idea that I was a working woman, because I had kept that side of my life from my children. I had always told my children that I worked for Perkins or some other restaurant chain, they never questioned that; because our hours do vary doing that kind of work.

When I told my son what had happened to me in court, I cried myself to sleep night after night. My son said, "Mom, it's all right. I love you no matter what." He told me he was the only young man he knew who had opportunities he'd been given, like going to his high school prom in a limo. He said he had appreciation that I had given them all a great life.

Why were charged dismissed? I was so angry. The prosecutor had put my life on hold for the next three years in a case that never had a leg to stand on in the first place. They had tape-recorded the entire incident, in which I stated to him five different times that he couldn't get sex from me. They knew they couldn't make the charge stick.

I wanted my day in court, but I had to pick up what little pride I had left and move on with my life. I was ironic to me that prostitution is legal in Nevada and other places like New Orleans, as long as the ladies are tested regularly and use protection. If I had done the crime, then I must do the time. I would have willingly taken my punishment accordingly. On the other hand, if I didn't commit a crime, then why should I be punished for no wrongdoings?

I rest my case. Where was the legitimate charge of prostitution? Where was the body language that the prosecuting attorney accused me of? It never happened. How could I have committed prostitution with body language that never happened?

The first day of the hearing, while I was outside the courtroom I was offered a deal to plea not guilty. I had never been arrested before for anything, including prostitution and the prosecutor knew the case against me was weak. But why take a deal for a crime I never committed in the first place? I couldn't take their deal because I hadn't done anything wrong to confess to.

I was never placed under arrest, because nothing was ever proven. There was a tape of our entire conversation and five times I had informed the officer that I did nothing but massages. Many women are entrapped into saying they did something wrong when they actually haven't done anything but a massage.

When I was ticketed for prostitution, I didn't know what to say or do in court, because I knew I hadn't done what they said. The officer in question said I tried to get him to buy sex from me, and the only thing the prosecuting attorney kept saying in front of the jurors was that my body language said yes, but my mouth said no.

My stomach stayed upset because I kept everything to myself. The thoughts buried deep within my mind were driving me crazy. I was hurt more than I was angry about the situation, because I always looked at my work as a choice, especially about whom I would decide to go to the next level with.

I just wanted my children to have the best sort of life I could possibly afford to give them. I had stopped living in order that they might live. My life was a secret garden to them and I never unearthed my profession. I thought telling him that his mother had prostituted herself would destroy his respect for me. When I told my son I had something to tell him, the tears began to flow down my face and I couldn't stop them. What could I do to get through this moment?

Teddie said, "Mom, try not to hurt so deeply. Just try and explain to me what is wrong." I then told him quite a bit of my past, but never the true meaning as to what started me to working in the first place: the abuse in my childhood. I just shared with him the fact that I was what many would consider a working woman.

He said, "Mom, you have given me such a wonderful life, there is nothing that you could tell me that would change my love for you. Don't be ashamed. I'm not ashamed of what you had to do to give me a good life."

He loved me before and he loves me even more now, if that is possible. I felt as though I must find a way to bring a bad police officer to justice—just like I would have to face justice if I'd broken the law.

I called my daughter, who was twenty-six years old at the time, and told her about my bust. I had recently told her what I had been doing for a living and that I didn't ever want her to sell herself short. She was working for a group home for severely handicapped adults at the time. When I told her, she reacted like my son had.

My kids have always been proud of me as a mother, because I nurtured them and tried to be a good mother. I didn't tell my sixteen- or twelve-year-old sons about my past. I saw no reason at that point to tell my younger boys.

At the time of my arrest, I had been in therapy for a long time trying to rid myself of the fear of being violated again. It had been a long time since I had a panic attack. I was comfortable at my job before the crooked undercover officer. That is, as comfortable as one can be doing the kind of work I was doing. My therapist told me I wouldn't be a whole person until I gave up my profession. Well, now that had happened.

With the history I had of rape and incest as a child, I had learned to hide all of my burdens deep down within my soul. I built a shell around myself and I didn't let anything or anyone break that barrier—until a shady system destroyed my defenses. I felt as though I had worked through the hurt and pain of my stepmother's physical and mental abuse just to have the system destroy all the work I had accomplished. For whose benefit should I sweep my unlawful arrest under the rug? Can anyone answer that question for me?

I could go on and on about what should have been, but it doesn't seem as if anyone cares about helping a person who isn't willing to help him or herself. I decided to get through this trauma through diligence, because I was finally free of many of those ties that had bound me most of my life.

For a while, I thought about pleading my case against the officer with an attorney who wasn't afraid of the system, but the shame was too devastating. My attorney said it would be hard to convict an officer, but the judge said I would have won the case hands down. The judge had seen my attorney in court with another client and asked about me and how I was doing, because he saw how torn up I was during my trial.

They had the right to destroy my life and then tell me that they could recharge me within the next three years. I was told if they came back to the sauna and I was working, they didn't even have to get a massage and they could take me to jail. I was afraid of the consequences of working in the sauna. What fool would take a chance on ending up in jail for the next three years? I mustered up the courage to find another profession—and way of life.

15

A New Skin

Life after my bust was a whirlwind of change. First, I attended Summit Academy, a vocational school in St. Paul, and learned computer software applications for home and business. I was a role model student while in school. I then applied my newly learned skills as an assistant at a nonprofit organization that specializes in bringing together professional job developers, case managers, employment specialists and supportive housing developers who had a need to find housing and employment services for their participants. As part of my job, I facilitated monthly meetings with about forty-five people, many of who had never shared resources with other organizations, while many times they had been servicing the same participants.

After working at the nonprofit for six years, a group of people I had worked with in different capacities and I decided to create our own nonprofit organization to work with men, women and youth exiting correctional institutions and those fleeing domestic violence situations. We received a $10,000 grant from the

Greater Minneapolis Council of Churches to help build the organization. A part of the grant required that I take a yearlong leadership development course at Hamline University.

Presently, as a motivational presenter and educator, I try to share the value of this work with many groups in the Twin Cities and Minnesota. We try to go deep and share our experiences to let participants know that we have all gone through challenges in our lives. Not all of us have experienced the life of incarceration, but we have all created out own "cells" at some point of our lives.

I am no longer angry at the police officer who accused me of solicitation. I still don't agree with the way I was falsely accused and dragged through the court system, but the event itself was the catalyst I needed to change my life. If I could go back in time, I would thank the officer.

Throughout my transformation, the women at my church were very supportive and loving. The more I purged the darkness and let go, the freer I became. It was cleansing. After finally making the plunge into my new life, I never looked back. I needed to surrender everything, so the Holy Spirit could come in and transform me. For me, it was Jesus, but I'm open to whatever a person needs—Jesus, Allah, Buddha, your Higher Power. I am here to support you wherever you're at.

As women, we need to know that no matter what choices we are given, we must never feel ashamed of what we have done to protect and care for our children. No system or man has the right to abuse or use us.

Ladies, don't be a pawn for the system. Don't be forced into admitting something that didn't happen. Our justice system and the U.S. Constitution say that we have certain rights as citizens of the United States, and my blood is red just like the rest of the people in this world. If you cut me, I bleed. I have feelings and emotions, too.

Admit it, ladies, we can pimp ourselves in the best interest of our children. They need us in their lives; our children remain in our lives even if a man decides to move on. Don't let anyone violate your body. We are the best violators of ourselves. We get beyond this through much work and with an enhancement of our self-esteem.

I know together we can do this and I assist men, women and youth as they learn to implement the stages of change at their own individual levels and capacities to grow.

There are times in our lives when we must face the music and run with it. The rest of my life looks much brighter. Never look back. Press ahead with vigor and don't let anyone put you down. The future is the new tomorrow. Never stop. Never give up.

THE END

978-0-595-44723-7
0-595-44723-6

Printed in the United States
80225LV00005B/25-138